FLORIDA

**Written by Carole Chester
Peace and Quiet section by
Paul Sterry**

© Automobile Association
Developments Limited 1995
First published 1990 as
Essential Florida
Reprinted 1990
Revised second edition 1992
Revised third edition 1995
Reprinted 1996; September
1997; March 1998
Reprinted as *Pocket Guide
Florida* 1999
Reprinted 2002, 2003

Maps © Automobile Association
Developments Limited 1995

Published and distributed in the
United Kingdom by AA
Publishing, a trading name of
Automobile Association
Developments Limited, whose
registered office is Millstream,
Maidenhead Road, Windsor,
Berkshire SL4 5GD.
Registered number 1878835.

A CIP catalogue record for this
book is available from the
British Library.

ISBN 0 7495 2119 8

The contents of this publication
are believed correct at the time
of printing. Nevertheless, the
publishers cannot be held
responsible for any errors or
omissions or for changes in the
details given in this guide or for
the consequences of any
reliance on the information
provided by the same. This
does not affect your statutory
rights. Assessments of
attractions, hotels, restaurants
and so forth are based upon the
author's own experience and,
there-fore, descriptions given in
this guide necessarily contain an
element of subjective opinion
which may not reflect the
publisher's opinion or dictate a
reader's own experience on
another occasion.

A01577

Colour separation: L C Repro
Ltd, Aldermaston

Printed by: Printer Trento srl,
Italy

Front cover picture: *Miami
Seaquarium* (AA Photo Library –
J Davison)

Contents

INTRODUCTION	4
BACKGROUND	7
WHAT TO SEE	9–100
MIAMI	9–28
THE KEYS	29–36
LEE ISLAND COAST	37–42
ORLANDO	43–54
THE PINELLAS	55–65
TAMPA	66–72
ELSEWHERE IN FLORIDA	73–100
PEACE AND QUIET: Countryside and Wildlife in Florida	101–109

FOOD AND DRINK	110
SHOPPING	112
ACCOMMODATION	114
NIGHTLIFE	114
WEATHER AND WHEN TO GO	115
CHILDREN	115
FESTIVALS AND EVENTS	116
HOW TO BE A LOCAL	118
TIGHT BUDGET TIPS	118
DIRECTORY	119–126
INDEX	127

Maps and Plans	
Locator	10
Miami and Miami Beach	19
Orlando	43
Tampa and St Petersburg	66–67
Florida	74–75

This book employs a simple rating system to help choose which places to visit:

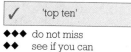

✓   'top ten'

◆◆◆ do not miss
◆◆ see if you can
◆ worth seeing if you have time

*Part of the Florida
magic: a ride
through the Magic
Kingdom in Walt
Disney World*

INTRODUCTION

Florida has many faces: the bright lights and
nightlife of Miami Beach, the laid back
bohemian atmosphere of the Keys, the sandy
beaches of the west coast, and the theme
parks of Orlando.

For tourists there are three great attractions:
the weather, the theme parks and the great
family value. Florida has a plethora of family
orientated amusement and entertainment
complexes – Walt Disney World being the
best known. Florida also boasts the lowest
car rental rates in the US – a factor that has
helped produce a wide variety and range of
package holidays, including fly/drive
programmes.

Florida, though a southern state, has always
stood apart from the rest of the 'deep south'.
In Miami you find a resort city which for
decades has featured top line performers in
its hotel supper clubs, and has been
patronised by the wealthy 'jet set' – all without
the benefit of casinos. Here there are beach-
fringed islands, loved by artists and writers,

fishermen and boating enthusiasts; there is also a wilderness which remained unexplored until the mid-19th century. Florida, surprisingly to many, is also rich in history. Within its boundaries are the two oldest European settlements in America (St Augustine and Pensacola), which date back to the 16th century, long before the Pilgrim Fathers reached the continent. In the historic northeast there are many state parks, several game management areas and a national forest. There are rivers and countless lakes and a beach made famous by racing cars. Racing, too, is a focal point of the central east coast, an area which also gave birth to the Kennedy Space Center.

The southeast is Florida's 'Gold Coast', a riviera where a string of resort communities and marinas have blossomed; yet the 200-mile (320-km) stretch of shoreline embraces two national parks and many state parks besides.

In the heartland of the state there is variety and adventure. This is fruit country, lake country, cattle country, horse country and fun country. The west coast's sunbelt resorts are called the Pinellas and the region encompasses no less than 12 state recreational areas and a state forest. Finally, the northwest offers the Florida Panhandle, a narrow strip of sand and salt marshes where magnolias and mossy oaks grow.

Florida is a springboard to the Caribbean, by air or luxury cruise liner, but within the state you will need to hire a car. There is accommodation to suit everyone, from super-expensive hotels, to budget self-catering apartments and villas by beach or golf course, to casual guest houses.

This is the sunshine state, where outdoor life has been developed for the holidaymaker's delight. Huge resorts with golf courses; racetracks for horses, greyhounds and cars; houseboats, yachts and canoes, are all on offer. Florida is a place where you have ample opportunity to see the sights, take up sports – or just relax.

If the pace is hurried at all, it is at Walt Disney World and the adjacent EPCOT, both still growing, and offering so many alternatives that even a week here is not long enough. The Disney-MGM film studios are the latest attraction and in the themed guest portion visitors can watch much of the production as it happens. The Studio Tour takes them through backlot streets, into sound stages where they can see the action from second floor soundproofed walkways and alongside post-production crafts, wardrobe and animation departments.

But Florida is not only beaches and theme parks – it has huge areas of unspoiled countryside where wildlife thrives; the Everglades is the most famous of these and, of course, there are many others. So, if you want to get back to nature, or just have a yen to see an alligator, then Florida is the place for you. Juan Ponce de León, a Spanish adventurer, came to Florida in 1513 in search of the legendary Fountain of Youth. He didn't find it back in the 16th century, but perhaps if he were one of today's travellers he might have pronounced the Spanish equivalent of *Eureka*!

Spaceship Earth, at Walt Disney World's EPCOT, takes visitors on a journey in time

BACKGROUND

Look at a map of Florida and one of the first things you may notice is the number of Indian place names.

At the time of Spanish exploration there were around 10,000 native Indians in Florida, divided into four tribes: the Timucuan and the Apalachees who lived in the central and northern territories, and the more aggressive Calusa and Mayimi in the south. But Florida is best known for the Seminoles (a name which means 'runaways'), originally Creek Indians from Georgia, who broke from their tribe and took over this area.

Their ranks were swelled by runaway slaves and by the 18th century they had formed a strong federation and occupied some of the best land in the interior. They caused little trouble to British settlers, having been offered land grants by British financiers, but when Florida was ceded back to Spain after the Revolutionary War, there were many clashes. Once the Americans decided they wanted the land for themselves, violent outrages occurred, especially as the US tried to move the Indians west of the Mississippi. Before long, 'incidents' of outrage and revenge became more frequent and developed into a war; several wars, in fact. The Seminole Wars lasted for seven years and cost a lot of lives and money. The Indian chiefs fought bravely but achieved little in territorial terms and today they are only

'The Great Spirit', a reminder of Indian history in modern Miami

remembered by place names; for example, Osceola, one of their great leaders, gives his name to a national forest. Those Indians who were not captured, killed or sent north, fled deeper into the interior, to what is now called the Everglades. Their descendants even now live in Florida in one of two recognised local tribes. Florida like its southern neighbours, has in the past been a slave-owning state boasting cotton and sugar plantations and by 1860 cotton was the basis of the state's economy. When Florida and its neighbours seceded from the Union in 1861 it became the main food supplier for the

BACKGROUND

southern army. But there is little of the Old South mentality here today. What is most noticeable is resort development, for which the weather and the railway may be thanked. Two far-sighted developers, Henry Flagler and Henry B Plant, made the first steps in the 1880s paving the way for what was to become a year-round holiday state. Henry Flagler, for instance, convinced of the site's tourist potential, built the pioneer hotel in Palm Beach – the Royal Poinciana and it was soon patronised by wealthy eastern seaboard society. He proved to be right, for Palm Beach continues to be an oasis of luxury on Florida's east coast. Whilst Flagler was busy on the east coast, Henry B Plant realised the potential in the western portion of the state and built the Tampa Bay Hotel in Tampa. But it wasn't until 1897 that Miami was able to open a plush hotel, the million-dollar Royal Palm, at a time when Miami Beach was just a mosquito-infested swampy island between the ocean and Biscayne Bay.

In many ways, it is difficult to come to terms with America's history, and Florida is a prime example. The Spanish may have discovered it in the 16th century, but it took decades more before development really meant anything. It wasn't, for example, until after World War I that real estate became big business in this part of the country. As with all such 'finds', reports of profits and quick fortunes soon attracted the speculators.

Between 1920 and 1930,

Florida's population quadrupled, seeing faster growth than in any other state. Overnight, cheap land was expensive, former paupers became millionaires. The Depression put paid to all that, but Florida did recover in the 1930s, when paper mills were introduced and refrigeration plants allowed the best local produce fruit and veg – to be more widely marketed. Farming turned co-operative and the citrus industry was regulated by law. Building resumed and Florida became a popular winter holiday destination for sunseekers from New York and the cold towns of the north.

Florida's image as an international vacation playground is far more recent, and for this we can thank developers such as Disney, as well as preservationists who have kicked life back into faded and neglected areas like the Art Deco district of Miami Beach and Tampa's Ybor City district. We can thank entrepreneurial airlines for introducing Tampa as an alternative gateway, showing us parts of the state that up until a few years ago were a local secret. Nowadays, one doesn't have to traipse to the Caribbean to discover a sand-fringed offshore island where the sun is warm and the water blue. The 'Sunshine State' gives a warm welcome to visitors and most attractions, such as theme parks, are open all week unless otherwise indicated. Museums, however, are generally closed on Sunday mornings.

MIAMI

Miami is a city of palm trees, warm sand and blue seas, yet it's also a cosmopolitan city full of banks and sky-high complexes. Here you can enjoy waterfront restaurants, marinas, pastel-coloured hotels, a boardwalk, and discover shopping malls, museums, an arts centre – and traffic jams. This is both a holiday and business destination, with sub-tropical foliage and an international clientèle. Miami is Florida's most sophisticated and busiest gateway.

Modest beginnings

Miami means many things. It means downtown, it means 'the Beach', it means the neighbourhoods like Coral Gables and the island of Key Biscayne. To understand what is where, it is necessary to understand Miami's

Miami Beach – 10 miles (16km) of white sands along the Atlantic

development. It was a determined woman by the name of Julia Tuttle who sent Henry Flagler frost-free orange blossoms from Biscayne Bay when the 'Big Freeze' of 1894 had destroyed most of the rest of Florida's citrus and vegetable crops. Her point was simply this: bring the railway south beyond Palm Beach and see – the weather is fine. Flagler understood perfectly, and in 1896, the railway link was completed and began to bring in materials and people. Miami was growing into a city. By 1899, the old troops' parade ground was suddenly a golf course, electricity and the telephone arrived, and dredging allowed the harbour to accommodate large ships. Miami Beach, on the other hand, was the dream of horticulturist John Collins. He tried to grow fruit here, and dredged the canal from Indian Creek to Biscayne Bay as a transport route. Having failed to achieve this goal he turned his hand to creating a residential community. In 1913 the first proper link, a 2-mile (3-km) wooden bridge, joined the two growing communities. Now there was no looking back. Despite setbacks from hurricanes, the land boom raced ahead. In the 1920s southern Florida was where everyone wanted to be. Developer George Merrick planned Coral Gables; Hialeah racetrack opened; hotels were constructed; a new air service inaugurated. Even so, it wasn't until the 1940s that more causeways were built across Biscayne Bay, including the Rickenbacker to Key Biscayne. Much has happened since then

to strengthen and maintain Miami's position as a boom city and resort as well as a major convention destination. Transport systems have been improved and in the last few years vast investments have been made to inject the glamour back into Miami Beach.

Travel in the city

Today's Miami is easily accessible to travellers within and beyond the US. Its international airport welcomes some 24 million passengers each year and is within a 15-minute drive of downtown and 25 minutes from Miami Beach. Greater Miami and the Beaches cover 1¼ million acres (half a million hectares) but the transportation system makes it relatively easy to get around. A rental car is vital since Miami's attractions are widely scattered. (The regions are connected by major thoroughfares and causeways.) Miami's elevated Metrorail system runs from south of Dadeland Mall to downtown Miami, to northwest Dade County, and is connected to the downtown Metromover shuttle system. A flat-fare system includes free transfers between Metrorail and Metromover. Miami's port is large enough to accommodate the newest cruise ships and is easy to reach by bridge from downtown Miami's Bayfront Park, Biscayne Boulevard. A regular bus service operates into the city centre.

What to see

In every part of the city there is some new office block or resort hotel, and there are always plans for further development. Although downtown Miami has become an international business and financial hub, it is still attractive for visitors. Valuable acreage along Biscayne Bay remains parkland; Bayfront Park offers shady respite from urban bustle and honours prominent historic figures. This is the site of the John F Kennedy Memorial Torch of Friendship, with its perpetual flame. And from the Riverwalk you can see the glossy cruise liners glinting in the sun. Alternatively you can browse through Bayside with its speciality shops, market place and street entertainment. To the north, Bicentennial Park also fronts on to Biscayne Boulevard, providing a place to fish, cycle and picnic. And in Mediterranean-style José Marti Park you can walk beside the busy Miami River. Miami's skyline is ever-changing: landmark monoliths include the 55-storey Southeast Financial Center overlooking the bay, and the 47-storey Centrust office tower. Banks and high-rise condominiums shoot up along Brickell Avenue demonstrating startling state-of-the-art architectural styles amongst the palm trees.

If the city has been investing in its future, so has Miami Beach, which stretches over 10 miles (16km) along the Atlantic and is as wide as a football field is long. Having emerged from a slump period, it can once again claim to have one of the

In less than 100 years Miami has grown to be a major business centre

best and most exciting shorelines in the US. Walk along the beachfront promenade, a 2-mile (3-km) boardwalk between 21st and 46th Streets, to see it for yourself.

Miami's marina is one of the best locations for all kinds of aquatic activities: charter dive boats and sailboats, powerboats and sportfishing boats, glass-bottom boat rides and much more. Next door at the port you can watch the cruise ships; or you can listen to a concert in South Pointe Park where there are jetty promenades and observation towers, picnic pavilions and, for the more

energetic, a fitness course. Everything in Miami seems to be either new or revived. In the 1950s the hotels along Collins Avenue became legendary, and now they have found new fame after being refurbished to meet the needs of the 1990s traveller. The Art Deco District at the southern end of the Beach is once more of interest, and its preserved 1930s hotels are enjoying a renaissance. A walking tour of the area, introduced in 1990, is a good way to get a feel for the days when American flappers strolled the pavements of Lincoln Road.

Although residents refer to 'the Beach', there are in fact several beaches, all communities with their own names. Surfside, for example, is wedged between Miami Beach to the south and Bal Harbour to the north. Accommodation is likely to cost less here, but Surfside sits by its own broad 1-mile (1.6-km) beach and boasts a main shopping and dining area along Harding Avenue, bordered by flowers and palm trees. Bal Harbour is more prestigious, though less than 1 mile (1.6km) in size, with shops on a par with Rodeo Drive in Beverly Hills. Just north of Haulover Park, a resort area with 3 miles (5km) of white sand beaches calls itself Sunny Isles, and has its own host of attractions for visitors, including outdoor activities, hotels and shopping malls.

Greater Miami is very cosmopolitan as you will discover when sightseeing, dining or joining in the myriad festivities taking place all through the year. Bahamians who helped settle the village of Coconut Grove are the originators of the Miami Goombay Festival in June. Every March Little Havana hosts its own Hispanic festival – a Rio carnival in miniature. Haitians, too, have added their traditions to the Miami melting pot along with Germans (a resident Oktoberfest) and Italians (a resident Renaissance Fair) – see **Festivals and Events**, pages 116–17.

WHAT TO SEE

AMELIA EARHART PARK
119th Street and Lejeune Road
An agricultural theme park named after the famous aviator who took off on her last flight from Miami. An interesting place to relax.

ARCH CREEK PARK
NE 135th Street and Biscayne Boulevard
The museum in the park here in the north of Miami, contains artefacts of the prehistoric Tequesta Indians as well as million-year-old mastodon bones. There are also live animals and nature displays, and nature walks are conducted most days.
Admission is free.

ART DECO DISTRICT ✓

from 6th to 23rd Street between Jefferson Avenue and Miami Beach
The only US national historic district to be built in the 20th century, this district is where 800 or so buildings were designed in the art deco style and colours of the 1930s. Only ten years ago, this area of the Beach was a neighbourhood of run-down hotels with seedy nightclubs and undistinguished eating places. But in 1986, 14 hotels reopened their doors in restored splendour with sparkling decorative terrazzo floors, brass lift doors and mirrored walls. Landmarks include the 70-room Cardozo, originally designed in 1939 and used in the 1950s for Frank

Miami's art deco hotels have been restored to their 1930s glory

Sinatra's film *A Hole in the Head*. Visitors to the district these days will find open air markets, Jewish delicatessens, excellent bakeries and Latin cafés. Along Ocean Drive, the Leslie Hotel with its SoBe Café is fully restored; the Carlyle Hotel and grill and the Waldorf Towers with its popular Downstairs at the Waldorf are again packing in the customers; along with the Breakwater Hotel and its rendezvous, Gerry's Place. Ovo Nightclub, at the corner of Espanola Way and Collins Avenue, once housed the Warsaw Ballroom. It now features gourmet cuisine and a stylish disco. The old Cinema Theater on Washington Avenue was an art deco gem in its time. Careful renovation has given it new life, as Club 1235. Lincoln

Road has been revived as a pedestrianised shopping mall, and the old Colony Theater, built as a showcase for Paramount Pictures in the 1930s, is now a modern performing arts centre. Espanola Way, a 1920s relic when fantasy themes were at their height, once again resembles the Spanish Village it was intended to be. Further development recently provided an oceanfront prom, decorative paving, wider pavements and new landscaping.

Art deco made its debut in Paris in 1925, but most impressed America in 1933 at the Chicago World's Fair. The Miami Design Preservation League conducts Saturday morning tours of the district for a small charge, and the Art

Deco Welcome Center conducts tours daily except Sunday, leaving from 1001 Ocean Drive (tel: (305) 672 2014 for details). Special events frequently take place in the area, such as the annual January Art Deco Weekend.

BASS MUSEUM
2121 Park Avenue, Miami Beach
This superb fine art gallery, the cultural centrepiece of Miami Beach, houses a permanent collection of medieval, Renaissance, baroque and rococo works, including Rubens, Lautrec and Van Haarlem. Closed Monday.

BAYFRONT PARK
Biscayne Boulevard
This attractive bayside park includes an amphitheatre which can seat 20,000 for outdoor concerts and other events. Panoramic views, picnic pavilions, a café and restaurant add to the appeal of wide green spaces. Bayside Marketplace is the city's trendiest shopping and dining complex and surrounds the marina. From the marina, sightseeing boat and gondola rides are available and HMS *Bounty* (used in the original film *Mutiny on the Bounty*) is occasionally moored at Bayside. Magicians, strolling musicians and mime artists entertain here.

CALLE OCHO
SW 8th Street
They call this 30-block strip

'Little Havana' and it certainly reflects the influence of Cuban culture. This is the place to shop (even on a Sunday) for delicious pastries and sweet black coffee, to sample Latin cuisine and buy cigars. The small cigar factories where you can see the end product being hand rolled are among the few places that actually thank you for smoking!
The neighbourhood's Latin Quarter is Miami's answer to New Orleans' French Quarter. It combines shops and restaurants, flower stalls and strolling musicians, and stretches as far as 7th Street and 17th Avenue.
A fiesta air is often prevalent along Calle Ocho (Spanish for 8th Street) and no more so than every March when the entire Hispanic community throws a street party for everyone.

CAULEY SQUARE
22400 Old Dixie Highway, Homestead
This 10-acre (4-hectare) historic railroad village is an example of typical 1920s Spanish style architecture. The two-storey complex – a building of thick stucco walls and coral rock – now houses a variety of boutiques, art galleries and craft shops. It includes an ice cream parlour and children's party centre, and is perhaps more designed for browsers than for serious shoppers. Annual festivals highlighting regional crafts and foods are held here every March, July and November. Closed Sunday.

MIAMI

◆◆◆
COCONUT GROVE
Bird Road (north), Le Jeune (west), Biscayne Bay (east) and Edgwater Drive (south)

Only a 10-minute drive from Downtown, 'the Grove' is Miami's most fashionable quarter, famous for its exclusive boutiques, restaurants and hotels. But perhaps best known is the Playhouse – a film theatre famous for many years and now the home of South Florida's leading resident professional theatre company.

The district is always lively, ultra-chic, and has earned the adjective 'Europeanised' from its pavement cafés, tiny bistros and pavement art shows. This is definitely *the* place to 'be seen'. Shoppers should visit Mayfair-in-the-Grove, the Main Highway, Fuller Street, Grand Avenue and Commodore Plaza. Nightclubs offer a great variety of sounds including jazz, country and western and reggae. They may well be tucked away in side streets and arcades, so it's worth exploring. Walking around the Grove is really the best way to discover the area, but a daily shuttle operates between Metrorail's Grove station and the hotels and attractions.

Don't miss the **Barnacle** on the Main Highway. This was the home of Ralph Middleton Munroe, an early pioneer, and is now a state historic site and museum, with beautifully landscaped grounds and a low entrance price. **Vizcaya** (see page 23) and the **Museum of Science and Space Transit Planetarium** (see page 22) are also located in this district. Coconut Grove is a diverse and lively community, and can be seen at its best during festival times. The three-day February Arts Festival attracts crowds to the streets to see artisans' work and to taste the local delicacies being offered. The June Goombay Festival is a Bahamian celebration; and the King Mango Strut in December is an 'anything goes' jamboree. Sport is important too; at the Dinner Key Marina on the Bay, you can rent sailboats and windsurfers or charter fishing boats. This Key used to be Pan Am's seaplane landing base and terminal, and was extremely busy in the 1930s and 1940s.

Italianate splendour in the East Loggia of the Vizcaya mansion

CORAL CASTLE
28655 South Dixie Highway, Homestead

A very strange but fascinating arrangement of coral rock sculptures and buildings, constructed between 1920 and 1940 by a Latvian immigrant for a woman who jilted him the day before they were to be married. He worked the 1,000 tons (1,016 tonnes) of coral here single-handedly and to this day no-one knows how he did it. Twenty five miles (40km) south of Miami on US1

CORAL GABLES

An élite residential district designed by George Merrick in the 1920s in Mediterranean style. Through coral rock gates and archways you may catch a glimpse of some of Miami's most desirable properties. Indeed, architectural standards are still strictly controlled to protect this garden area's beauty, and the boulevards, overlooked by leafy banyans, palms and poincianas, are well maintained.

It was in this area that the University of Miami was founded, and a variety of campus activities keeps the Gables lively. There is also good theatre, first class dining in restaurants which reflect the city's international air, and plenty of interesting shops, including those along the celebrated 'Miracle Mile'. Bus tours are given of the Gables but it is equally easy to take the 20-mile (32-km) self-guided tour prepared for visitors by the city. Pick up a free map and start at the gateway to the Gables, **La Puerta del Sol**. Merrick erected this 90-foot (27-m) belltower and 40-foot (12-m) arch and put it on the National Register of Historic Places. Among the district's attractions is Merrick's boyhood home, **Coral Gables Merrick House**, 907 Coral Way, for which the city was named. The house was originally constructed in 1898, of locally quarried coal. It is furnished in 'twenties' style, with many Merrick family pieces. (Open Sunday and Wednesday afternoons only.) Another sight in the city of Coral Gables is the **Venetian Pool**. This exotic lagoon is a natural spring-fed pool carved from coral rock in 1923 and enhanced with palms, islands, caves, waterfalls and arched bridges. It is very popular with children in summer.

The Gables is not lacking in museums. **Lowe Art Museum**, located on the University campus, is the county's oldest for visual arts and is distinguished by its Kress collection of Old Masters. The collections of southwest American Indian art and textiles are worth seeing too. (Closed Monday.)

Fairchild Tropical Gardens (see page 18) are well worth visiting, and a novel way to tour the district is to rent a bicycle and take advantage of the miles of special bike paths which loop through shaded streets down the Old Cutler Road Bikeway to Matheson Hammock Country Park. Coral Gables is close to Downtown.

◆◆
FAIRCHILD TROPICAL GARDENS

Old Cutler Road, Coral Gables
A favourite stop on most itineraries, these gardens are said to have the country's largest subtropical botanical variety, with over 80 acres (32 hectares) of palms, cycads and other exotic plants from around the world. You can take the winding paths through a rain forest, the Vine Pergola, Sunken Garden, Palm Glade and Rare Plant House and around eight lakes, or opt for one of the guided tram tours.

◆
FLAMINGO PARK

1245 Michigan Avenue, Miami Beach
This is the place for tennis lovers. The tennis complex comprises clay and hard courts, many of them lit for night matches, and tournaments are frequently held in the 5,000-seat Abel Holtz Stadium. There are also other recreational facilities on offer here, including a swimming pool.

◆
FREEDOM TOWER

600 Biscayne Boulevard
Inspired by the Giralda Tower in Seville (Spain), it was built in 1925 to house the Miami Daily News. It changed its name in the 1960s when it became the Cuban Refugee Emergency Center. Closed to the public.

◆
FRUIT AND SPICE PARK

24801 SW 187th Avenue, Homestead
An unusual botanical park, featuring, as its name suggests, fruits and spices from around the globe – in all more than 200 species and 500 varieties, set in 20 acres (8 hectares). Of particular interest is the demonstration herb and vegetable garden. Admission is free for those who want to tour on their own but a small charge is made for a guided tour (by request). It is 35 miles (56km) southwest of Miami, off US1.

◆
GOLD COAST RAILROAD & MUSEUM

12450 SW 152nd Street
A 'working' railway museum whose displays include presidential cars, steam and diesel locomotives. Visitors may also take the 3½-mile (5-km) half-hour trip on a 1913 steam train. The museum opens daily, but train rides are available only at weekends.

A vivid Bird of Paradise flower in the Fairchild Tropical Gardens

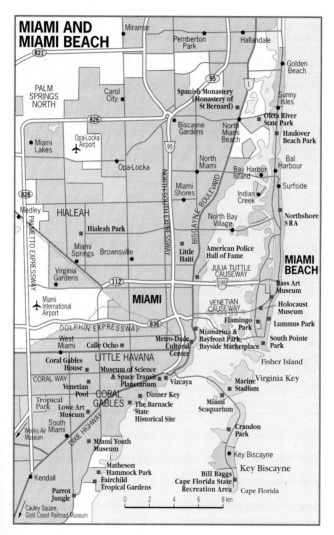

MIAMI AND MIAMI BEACH

◆
HAULOVER PARK
10800 Collins Avenue
This popular recreation area is a good spot for surfing, and has an ocean-front pier for fishing and a marina where boats may be rented. It also includes a nine-hole golf course.

HIALEAH PARK
Okeechobee Road
The Miami Canal separates this sporting district from its sister city, Miami Springs. The Hialeah Racetrack is one of the biggest draws, though people like to visit its park site outside the horse-racing season to enjoy the superbly landscaped grounds. An aquarium, aviary and a famous flock of uncaged flamingos add to the attraction. Another reason to visit Hialeah is the Miami Jai-Alai fronton (stadium) the country's oldest and largest arena for the very popular old Basque game, where a *pelota* (a very hard ball) is hurtled around a court at speeds of up to 188mph (241 kph); it is enjoyed by spectators who can bet on teams or individual players, or merely watch the action over dinner in the clubhouse.

KENNEDY PARK
South Bayshore Drive and Kirk Street, Coconut Grove
Popular with joggers or for a work-out on the Vita course; and just for fun there's a 'frisbee golf' course.

KEY BISCAYNE
The peaceful pine groves and semi-tropical beaches on this beautiful island ('key' means island), so close to Downtown, make a perfect retreat from the more fashionable sands and bronzed bodies of Miami Beach. In the 1940s, when the causeway was constructed, urban dwellers began to realise the potential of this island as a weekend retreat. Today there are private homes, hotels, business operations and many sport facilities in this somewhat secluded setting.

At one end of the island, **Crandon Park** is favoured by golfers and picnickers. At the southern tip of Key Biscayne, the smaller **Bill Baggs Cape Florida State Recreation Area** is also an area for outdoor enjoyment. Here, Cape Florida Lighthouse was built in 1825, and now houses a historical museum. It is South Florida's oldest landmark, survivor of both the Seminole Wars and the Civil War. Don't miss a visit to America's largest aquatic park, **Biscayne National Underwater Park**. A glass-bottomed boat is the only way to explore 181 acres (73 hectares) of colourful reefs, home to numerous species of tropical fish, but you can leave the boat to snorkel or scuba dive. **Virginia Key**, an island just north of Key Biscayne, is where you will find the **Miami Marine Stadium**, venue for international rowing events and summer pop concerts. Also here is the **Miami Seaquarium** (see page 22). Reach both islands on Rickenbacker Causeway.

LUMMUS PARK
between 5th and 14th Street, Miami Beach
Free beach concerts are often held here and you can rent umbrellas and watersport equipment in this grassy, palm-lined park next to the beach.

Windsurfing is popular on Key Biscayne, a stone's throw from Miami

◆◆
METRO-DADE CULTURAL CENTER
101 West Flagler Street
If the weather is dull, this complex in the heart of Downtown is the place to visit. Built in a Mediterranean style around a plaza high above Flagler Street, it covers a complete city block and embraces a library and two museums. Entrance to the **Center for the Fine Arts** is by covered walkway from the central plaza. In addition to an auditorium and exhibition space, there are two floors of main galleries and a sculpture court, which house high quality changing exhibitions.
The **Historical Museum of Southern Florida** is highly recommended for an introduction to the area and includes several hands-on exhibits which tell the 10,000-year story of man in this region. Closed Sunday mornings, open late on Thursday evenings.

◆◆◆
METROZOO
Coral Reef Drive and SW 124th Avenue
Miami's main zoo is one of the most modern cageless types in the USA. It is home to some 100 species, including white tigers and rhinos, and spreads over 225 acres (90 hectares). Many of the animals are kept in near-natural habitats, separated from visitors by moats. Wings of Asia is a free-flight aviary with 300 tropical birds.
Monorail tours give an overall view, but boats and elephants

are also available as transport, and the petting zoo is ideal for small children. Take the Florida Turnpike or US1 to SW 152nd Street and follow the signs.

♦♦
MIAMI MUSEUM OF SCIENCE AND SPACE TRANSIT PLANETARIUM
3280 S Miami Avenue, Coconut Grove
An educational museum which manages to be fun, this one explores the worlds of light, sound, energy, biology and much more with over 140 hands-on exhibits and computer games. Multi-media and laser shows are given in the planetarium and, weather permitting, star gazing is free on weekend evenings in the Weintraub Observatory. Also look in at the Animal Exploratorium, where reptiles

Dolphins are put through their paces in the Miami Seaquarium

and local marine life may be handled. Great for children.

♦♦♦
MIAMI SEAQUARIUM
Virginia Key, via Rickenbacker Causeway
Highly recommended for all the family, who can spend an action-packed day here. Dolphins, sealions and killer whales all have starring roles in shows given several times a day. Tanks displays include rare tropical fish. There are tropical gardens and a wildlife sanctuary.

♦
MIAMI YOUTH MUSEUM
Bakery Centre, 5701 Sunset Drive
This hands-on cultural arts centre is designed to encourage youngsters to appreciate art by creating their own visual and musical effects. Admission free for under 4's. Closed mornings Tuesday to Thursday.

♦
MICCOSUKEE INDIAN VILLAGE
Tamiami Station
Aimed primarily at tourists; children will no doubt enjoy the alligator wrestling, even if they are not interested in the exhibits of tribal patchwork and basketry. The museum displays films and artefacts from many Indian tribes. Take US41; about 30 miles (48km) west of Miami.

♦♦♦
MONKEY JUNGLE
14805 SW 216th Street, South Miami
Here you can walk along a

caged pathway through a near-natural rain forest, while the monkeys swing free. They have even more avid curiosity than their visitors, and their antics are highly entertaining. Gorillas, orangutans and the tiniest monkeys can be seen, but the stars are the clever chimps. Recommended for children. Admission free for under 5's. Reached via US1.

THE ORIGINAL ORCHID JUNGLE
26715 SW 157th Avenue, Homestead
This natural Florida jungle is where the loveliest of orchids from around the world grow. Wander at will along one of the jungle trails. Twenty five miles (40km) south of Miami; reached via US1.

◆◆◆
PARROT JUNGLE AND GARDENS
11000 SW 57th Avenue
A perennial favourite and one of Florida's oldest and best developed attractions. Although most of the birds are caged, hundreds of brilliantly coloured tropical birds fly freely, sometimes perching on your shoulder. There are also 2,000 varieties of plants and flowers growing here. One highlight is the trained bird show in the Parrot Bowl, where cockatoos and macaws do a high wire act, skate and perform a number of other tricks. Flamingo Lake is spectacular with its 75 pink Caribbean flamingos. Recommended for children.

◆◆
SOUTH POINTE PARK
Government Cut
This 17-acre (7-hectare) park, at the southern end of Miami Beach, is the place to fish and watch the great liners head for the Port of Miami, the world's largest cruise ship port.

SPANISH MONASTERY
North Miami Beach
If it looks authentically Spanish, it should: it was first erected in Spain in the 12th century, and brought piecemeal to America in 1925. The monastery of St Bernard houses antiques and works of art. Open to the public.

◆◆◆
VIZCAYA
3251 South Miami Avenue, Coconut Grove
Once the home of James Deering, founder of International Harvesters, this 70-room Italianate mansion sits in 10 acres (4 hectares) of formal gardens overlooking Biscayne Bay. Lavishly decorated, it is a treasure house of European art. A Shakespeare Festival and an Italian Renaissance Fair are both held in the grounds.

WEEKS AIR MUSEUM
14710 SW 128th Street, Tamiami Airport
A museum dedicated to the preservation of aircraft from their beginnings through World War II. More than 35 aircraft (many restored to flying condition) are on display.

Accommodation

There is a multitude of world-class hotels, budget-price hotels and holiday apartments in the Miami area.

The following are some recommended hotels in the top bracket:

Alexander All-Suite Luxury Hotel, 5225 Collins Avenue, Miami Beach (tel: (305) 865 6500). A plush oceanfront hotel where all 206 rooms have suites with their own kitchen. Hotel facilities include dining room, cocktail lounge, entertainment, swimming pools, tennis courts and golf course privileges.

Biscayne Bay Marriott Hotel & Marina, 1633 North Bayshore Drive (tel: (305) 374 3900). A Downtown bayfront 605-room hotel connected by skywalk to Omni International Shopping Mall. Three restaurants and lounges plus pool, sauna and whirlpool.

Doral Ocean Beach Resort, 4833 Collins Avenue, Miami Beach (tel: (305) 532 3600). A long established and recently revived 420-room beachfront hotel. Guest rooms are delightful, if costly, as are the dining room and pleasant coffee shop. Other facilities include gardens, swimming pool, tennis courts, aqua club, and a golf course at the Doral Resort & Country Club near the airport.

Fontainebleau Hilton Resort, 4441 Collins Avenue, Miami Beach (tel: (305) 538 2000). This long established beachfront hotel with 1,206 rooms is enormous but beautifully laid out. Landscaping includes a rock grotto free-form swimming pool. There are 14 restaurants and lounges to choose from, including dining al fresco, and a nightclub where many top names perform. Many sports facilities.

Grand Bay Hotel, 2669 South. Bayshore Drive, Coconut Grove (tel: (305) 858 9600). A plush 181-room European-style hotel overlooking Biscayne Bay in an attractive garden setting. Facilities include health club, swimming pool, sauna and whirlpool, an elegant restaurant and the prestigious Regine's nightclub.

Sheraton Bal Harbour, 9701 Collins Avenue (tel: (305) 865 7511). A 675-room hotel in a glamorous beachfront location. Rooms have kitchenettes. There are nine restaurants, lounges, and a supper club noted for musical revues. Other facilities include two pools, sauna, whirlpool and tennis.

In the Art Deco District, several smaller hotels have been restored and are particularly popular, notably: the **Carlyle**, 1250 Ocean Drive (tel: (305) 532 5315); **Waldorf Tower**, 860 Ocean Drive (tel: (305) 531 7684); **Edison**, 960 Ocean Drive (tel: (305) 531 0461); and **Park Central**, 640 Ocean Drive (tel: (305) 538 1611).

In Sunny Isles, reasonably priced hotels include: **Chateau-By-The-Sea** and **Driftwood Resort Motel**, 17121 Collins Avenue (tel: (305) 944 5141). Also recommended in this area is **Radisson Pan-American**

Hotel, 17875 Collins Avenue (tel: (305) 932 1100). **Mayfair House**, Florida Avenue, Coconut Grove (tel: (305) 441 0000), is rather unusual; all 185 suites feature their own jacuzzi and often an upright (antique) piano. **The Biltmore** in Coral Gables is one of the city's best-known hotels, with a long history of catering to the rich and famous. It was built in 1926 and, like the downtown Freedom Tower, it was modelled on the Giralda, Seville Cathedral's bell tower. Even if you can't afford to stay here, a visit is worthwhile for afternoon tea, or to join a free historical walk, every Sunday at 13.30, 14.30 and 15.30hrs (tel: (305) 445 1926). **The Inter-Continental**, 100 Chopin Plaza (tel: (800) 332 4246 toll free), famous for its collection of priceless tapestries is also recommended. Another option is the **Sheraton Royal Biscayne Beach Resort & Racquet Club**, 555 Ocean Drive, Key Biscayne (tel: (305) 361 5775). A glamorous oceanfront resort with its own private beach. Good sport facilities include two pools and ten tennis courts.

Children
There are many family attractions in the Miami area which are ideal for children. Novel animal shows are presented at Monkey Jungle and Parrot Jungle and, of course, the dolphins and whales are the stars at Miami Seaquarium. Exotic species are on view at the Metrozoo. In the US, museums are never dull. Of special note are the Museum of Science and Space Transit Planetarium, and the South Florida Historical Museum, both of which have many hands-on exhibits (see also **What to see**).

A flock of flamingos in the pink at Parrot Jungle

MIAMI

Restaurants

When it comes to eating in Miami you're truly spoilt for choice. A vast range of ethnic cuisine is available, and fast food outlets are innumerable. (Consult *The Greater Miami Menu Guide*, a dining and entertainments listing from news-stands and certain hotels.) Among the hotel restaurants recommended are:

Dominique's, Alexander Hotel, 5225 Collins Avenue, Miami Beach (tel: (305) 865 6500). Serving excellent French food in a romantic setting. The pink and green dining room is enhanced by Oriental rugs and antique furniture.

Restaurant Place St Michel, Hotel Place St Michel, 162 Alcazar Avenue, Coral Gables (tel: (305) 444 1666). A café atmosphere for French cuisine, breakfast, lunch and dinner. Good Sunday brunch with a champagne buffet.

Veronique's, Biscayne Bay Marriott, 1633 North Bayshore Drive (tel: (305) 374 3900). Gourmet setting for *haute cuisine* and local seafood. First class (and expensive) service includes at-table presentations.

Non-hotel restaurants worth looking at include:

Casa Juancho, 2436 SW 8th Street (tel: (305) 642 2452). In the heart of Little Havana, this upmarket restaurant features regional Spanish cuisine, plus a *tapas* menu, and strolling *mariachi* musicians. Jacket and tie required.

Chart House Restaurant, 51 Chart House Drive, Coconut Grove (tel: (305) 856 9741).

Features American favourites: steak and prime rib, oysters and seafood dishes; there is also a salad bar. Cut costs with cocktails and appetizers on one of the outside decks overlooking Biscayne Bay.

Dockside Terrace, Bayside Marketplace, 401 Biscayne Boulevard (tel: (305) 358 6419). Casual waterfront spot with a good view of the Marketplace and marina. Seafood is a speciality either indoors or out on the terrace.

East Coast Fisheries Restaurant, 360 W Flagler Street (tel: (305) 373 5515). Long-established seafood restaurant on the Miami River. The first floor doubles as fish market and dining room so you can be sure the seafood is fresh.

Joe's Stone Crab, 227 Biscayne Boulevard, Miami Beach (tel: (305) 673 0365). Something of an evergreen, this has been operating since 1913. Large, noisy and casual; the seafood is delicious. Pick a platter of stone crabs and dip them in butter or mustard sauce. Closed mid-May to mid-October and Sunday and Monday lunchtime.

Euro Pub, 790 NE 79th Street (tel: (305) 754 2678). Cosy, European-style pub, offering traditional dishes from Ireland, France, Italy, Austria, Hungary and Germany.

Shopping

Elegant speciality shops, indoor and outdoor malls and genuine street markets can be found all over Miami. There's a wonderful variety including neighbourhood and ethnic

Bayside Marketplace is Miami's most entertaining shopping complex

shops as well as designer boutiques and discount stores. Below is a selection of some of the best and most interesting places for visitors to see – even if only to enjoy the surroundings and window-shop:

Aventura Mall, 19501 Biscayne Boulevard, North Miami Beach. Expansive two-level mall with over 200 stores and 21 eating places. In addition to boutiques and antique stores, there are major department stores such as Macy's and Lord & Taylor. Aventura is most easily reached from Dade and Broward counties.

Arthur Godfrey Road, east of the Julia Tuttle Causeway. The main thoroughfare from the airport to the Beach is one of the main shopping streets, easily reached on foot from many of the beachfront hotels. It is an old street but a flourishing one.

Bakery Center, South Miami.

Multi-million dollar complex with many fine speciality stores, international restaurants and cinemas. Unusual artwork surrounds it, including Jonathan Borofsky's 24-foot (7-m) *Hammering Man* and illusionary murals by Richard Haas.

Bal Harbour, Collins Avenue at 97th Street. An exclusive shopping area in a beautifully designed garden setting with blossoming orange trees, tropical foliage and ferns. Saks Fifth Avenue and Neiman-Marcus are the department store 'anchors' to this three-level open-air mall.

Bayside Marketplace, 401 Biscayne Boulevard. The city's finest shopping attraction: a two-storey speciality centre which encompasses 140 shops, restaurants and pavilions surrounding Miamarina at Biscayne Bay. Fashions, handicrafts and Latin American food stalls all feature.

Cutler Ridge Mall, 20505 South Dixie Highway, Cutler Ridge. Over 170 shops, including major department stores such as Lord & Taylor, Burdines, Jordan Marsh, Sears and J C Penney.

Dadeland Mall, 7535 North Kendall Drive, Kendall. Popular and busy. Anchor department stores are Jordan Marsh, Burdines, Saks Fifth Avenue and Lord & Taylor, but there are also speciality shops. Metrorail stops conveniently near by.

The Falls, 8888 Howard Drive, Kendall. An outdoor mall with landscaped walkways, waterfalls and bridges, featuring a range of speciality shops and restaurants. Stores include Miami's only branch of Bloomingdale's.

Flagler Street A bustling street at the heart of downtown with all types of shops including Burdines.

Hallandale Flea Market, Gulfstream Race Track and Hallandale Beach Boulevard. A good place to browse for new and secondhand goods, but it's only open at weekends.

Lincoln Road Mall, 16th Street and Lincoln Road, Miami Beach. Once the most popular place to shop, until all the others came along. Still holding its own, the mall has 175 stores lining an open air pedestrianised zone where only electric trams operate. This mall is sometimes referred to as the International Market Place.

Little Havana, SW 8th Street (Calle Ocho) and W Flagler Street. Sells all things Cuban. Particularly good for cigars.

Loehmann's Plaza, Biscayne Boulevard at 187th Street, North Miami Beach. Discount stores are particularly worth looking for, selling designer label items.

The Mall at 163rd Street, North Miami Beach. Three-level complex boasting around 150 speciality shops as well as major department stores such as Burdines and Jordan Marsh.

Mayfair in the Grove, 2911 Grand Avenue, Coconut Grove. Exclusive atrium-styled promenade where you can find the likes of Yves St Laurent and Ralph Lauren fashions, as well as elite restaurants and nightclubs.

Miami Fashion District, NW 5th Avenue, and 22nd Street. Shops featuring clothes and home accessories.

Miracle Mile, SW 24th Street, Coral Gables. Almost anything you might want is to be found in the 150 or so stores along this tree-lined thoroughfare. Miracle Center has 50 specialist shops, a cinema, restaurants and nightclubs.

Omni International Mall, 1601 Biscayne Boulevard. Part of a downtown hotel and convention facility, this five-floor enclosed mall has numerous speciality shops, exclusive boutiques, department stores and restaurants. A covered walkway links the Omni International Mall to the Biscayne Bay Marriott Hotel & Marina.

THE KEYS

The Florida Keys are very special. This group of 45 islands, which the Spanish called *cayos*, is dotted in a 150-mile (240-km) arc from the southern tip of the mainland deep into the Gulf of Mexico. Actually, early explorers never stopped at any of the rocky outcrops, but referred to them as *Los Martires*, or 'The Martyrs', because they looked to them like suffering men rising from the sea. The native Indian inhabitants were left to hunt and fish in peace. In the 15th century the fierce Calusa tribe inhabited the Keys, but Indian mounds still visible these days suggest the earliest residents were the Arawaks and Caribees.

Pirates came and went but it wasn't until the 18th century that white settlers came to stay. For the most part they farmed – limes, tamarind and breadfruit, and in the Lower Keys, pineapples. Later, a thriving shark factory was established on Big Pine Key; the shark hides were sent north to be processed into a tough leather known as shagreen. Transplanted British loyalists and Yankee seafarers both arrived in the 19th century, followed by Cubans, who established cigar factories here.

It was only during this century that tourism reached the Keys. Once Henry Flagler extended his railroad from Miami to Key West in 1912, the wealthy were eager to enjoy the Keys'

One of the world's longest over-water roads links the Florida Keys

good climate and relaxed atmosphere. The railway was supplanted by an oversea highway in 1938 – a tremendous engineering feat now incorporating 42 bridges, including the largest of all, the Seven Mile Bridge. Travellers by road can reach Key West from Miami in three hours. It is possible to fly there, but it would be a shame to miss the scenery (blue lagoons, olive groves, white pines); the wildlife (herons, spoonbills, pelicans and osprey); and the beautiful crystal-clear waters surrounding the islands – the perfect location for fishing, diving, sailing and boating.

WHAT TO SEE

◆◆◆
KEY LARGO

This is the most northerly of the Keys, and is best known for **John Pennekamp Coral Reef State Park**, America's first underwater park, covering an area of some 75 square miles (194sq km). It is accessible from Miami in about an hour's drive (58 miles). Named after a Miami newspaper editor and conservationist, Pennekamp is a wonderful place for anyone with an interest in marine life. The waters are clear and calm; the underwater living world exotic and colourful. There are said to be around 650 species of fish and over 40 different varieties of coral, as well as many other marine creatures here.

There are four main ways to view Pennekamp, of which the glass-bottom boat is the easiest. Passengers are taken on a tour of Molasses Reef at the southern end of the park. This is also the most popular diving and snorkelling spot, for almost every kind of coral can be seen in one place.

Snorkelling can be done easily by anyone who can swim and a special boat leaves several times daily for 2½-hour reef trips, much of which time is actually spent in the water. A package price includes equipment and instruction. To join the dive boat, you do need to be a certified diver, though scuba instruction is available. Dive sites vary depending upon conditions but are likely to be Molasses Reef, French Reef or Benwood

Humphrey Bogart's haunt in **Key Largo** *was the Keys Caribbean Club*

Wreck. For man-made sights, try Dry Rocks, where a bronze statue of Christ is immersed in 20 feet (6m) of water. The Jules' Undersea Lodge provides overnight accommodation five fathoms below – write to POB 3330, Key Largo, FL 33037, for details.

Visitors looking for alternatives to the underwater attractions will find man-made beaches, canoe trails, nature trails and windsurfers for rent.

At Mile Marker 100 (MM 100) you can see the real *African Queen* from the film of the same name, which starred Humphrey Bogart and Lauren Bacall.

In October, Sands Key, Elliott Key and Old Rhodes Key in the Biscayne Waterway are the focal points for the annual

Columbus Day regatta. The tiny island between Elliott Key and Old Rhodes Key was once a pirate's stronghold known as Black Caesar's Rock. According to legend, Black Caesar was an escaped negro slave who pirated ships so well single-handedly that he became Blackbeard's trusty aide.

THE UPPER KEYS
Anywhere in this stretch of archipelago between Key Largo and Long Key is within easy reach by car from Miami. You may care to stop at **Tavernier Key**; ornithologists tour the Florida Bay Rookeries from here.

The island's name comes from pirate Jean Lafitte's associate Tavernier, who frequently used it as a hiding place in the 18th century. Many historic buildings have recently been restored.

ISLAMORADA
This popular Upper Keys base lies in the centre of a coral and palm-fringed group of islands colloquially known as 'the purple isles', comprising Plantation, Windley, Upper and Lower Matecumbe Keys and Long Quay. 'Purple' may refer to the concentration of violet sea snails (*janthina janthina*) found on the seashore here, though some say it is for the purple orchids and bougainvillaea that cover the islands.

There are first-class resorts, marinas, tennis and golf facilities at Islamorada – one of the first areas to provide a nature walk and bicycle pathway for tourists. It also has a reputation for being one of the finest fishing areas for tarpon and sailfish. Don't miss **Theater of the Sea**, where porpoises and sea lions cavort in large, coral rock-lined natural ponds. A 'Swim with a Dolphin' programme allows you to jump in with these fascinating marine animals (tel: (305) 664 2431 to book). The Theater also stages a show starring rays, turtles, sharks, sealions and dolphins. The 'purple isles' were a notable wreckers' headquarters in the early years of the 19th century, and around Mile Marker 78 (MM 78) at the San Pedro Underwater Park there is a wreck of a Spanish galleon off the coast.

Tiny **Lignumvitae Key** is

where some of the last remaining examples of the Key's original vegetation still grows. On this 280-acre (113-hectare) island there are several Lignumvitae ('wood of life') trees along with mahogany, strangler fig, poisonwood, pigeon plum and gumbo limbo trees. This is now a state park botanic site, with conducted tours. **Long Key** is recommended for snorkellers. Dive shops will arrange individual or group trips to the nearby reefs. In the town of Layton there is the **Zane Grey Creek** and the **Sea World Shark Institute** to explore, and nature trails in **Long Key State Recreation Area**.

THE MIDDLE KEYS

The section of the archipelago between Long Key and the Seven Mile Bridge mostly consists of small islands with names like Conch, Duck, Crawl and Grassy – the latter being named after an early settler, not the vegetation. **Marathon** is a well developed tourist centre in the Middle Keys, with its own airport, convention centre and golf course. It was once an escape hatch for such pirates as Henry Morgan and Jean Lafitte. On **Grassy Key** there's a **Dolphin Research Center** where the dolphins live in a natural environment, and educational tours inform the public about their lifestyle. Visitors can encounter them more closely by going swimming with them (tel: (305) 289 1121).

THE LOWER KEYS

This is the area between the Seven Mile Bridge and Key West. Largest of these Keys is:

BIG PINE KEY

Covered with silver palmetto, Caribbean pine and cacti, this tropical islet is famous for its handful of tiny key deer (little bigger than an average-sized dog) which once were plentiful throughout the Keys. Nowadays, the few that are left are protected here in the **National Key Deer Refuge**. If you see one, don't feed it as this will encourage it to stray near the road.

Six miles (10km) south of Big Pine Key is **Looe Key National Marine Sanctuary**, a magnificent coral reef providing an ideal spot for snorkelling and diving in anything from 2 to 40 feet (0.6 to 12m) of warm, clear Gulf Stream water. Access is by boat from the Bahia Honda State Recreation Area.

KEY WEST ✓

The most southerly and the best known Key. It boasts the most opulent resorts, most famous personalities, most colourful history and the most lively nightlife. The smugglers and the rum-runners loved it in the past, and a diverse set of people love it today. The busiest time to come is festival time.

In October the Fantasy Fest embraces Halloween and is Key West's answer to the *mardi gras*, with street fairs, arts and crafts shows, parades and floats and food festivals.

February brings the excitement of Old Island Days. At this time of year, private homes are lit up, and their owners invite the public inside; fun and games include a conch shell blowing contest, and many other festivities, which finish in March with the blessing of the local shrimp fleet. Although this celebration was only launched in 1960, it has become extremely popular; area captains now paint their vessels and deck them out with bunting for the occasion.

Summer visitors should make a note that the anniversary of former resident Ernest Hemingway's birth is 21 July, and this is commemorated with a week-long festival. A look-alike contest, short story and story telling contests, costume party and billfish tournament (a deep-sea fishing contest) are all included in what Key West calls 'Hemingway Days'.

Hemingway loved Key West and **Hemingway House** on Whitehead Street is now a museum, housing photographs and other memorabilia, including his typewriter and descendants of his cats. Guided tours, laced with Hemingway anecdotes, are given daily. The swimming pool here was the first in Key West.

Across the street is the **Lighthouse Military Museum**. Here visitors may climb to the top, peer through a submarine periscope and wander through half-an-acre (0.2 hectare) of military hardware. Displays

Ernest Hemingway's Key West home

include one of the two remaining 'two-man' submarines launched by the Imperial Japanese Navy during World War II.

Audubon House on Whitehead Street is associated with the noted artist and naturalist John James Audubon who visited the Keys in 1832. A well restored 1812 mansion, it was the home of salvager and harbour pilot Captain John Geiger, and is furnished in the period's style. Numerous original Audubon engravings are on view, many from his famous 'Birds of America' folio. During his visits, Audubon explored the mangroves in search of native birds, often starting out at 3am. You can take a guided tour or watch a video, showing the tremendous detail of his drawings.

The **Oldest House (Wreckers**

Museum) is located on Duval
Street, which is also the best
shopping and dining street. It
is an 1829 sea captain's house,
with the ship's hatch in the
roof showing the influence of
early shipbuilding. Many early
wooden houses featuring
intricate fretwork (known as
'gingerbread' style), with
railings and large verandas,
were built by ships'
carpenters. Inside there are
models of shops and a
furnished dolls' house.

The main rendezvous point is
Mallory Square, by the
waterfront – especially at
sunset. If you haven't seen a
Mallory Pier sunset you
haven't lived, or so they say,
and at this time of day the
square really comes alive with
tumblers, jugglers, string
quartets – and it is all free.
Here too is the **Key West
Aquarium**, the first open-air
aquarium to be built in the US
and the oldest attraction in the
Keys. You can see a living
coral reef, shark tanks and a
turtle pool. The 'touch tank'
contains creatures which may
safely be handled.

Turtle Kraals is in the shrimp
dock area and is home to
loggerhead turtles weighing
up to 400 pounds (180kg).
There is also a 'touch tank' for
children and an aviary. **Mel
Fisher Maritime Heritage
Society Museum** on Greene
Street displays millions of
dollars-worth of treasure –
gold and silver bars and
jewellery. They were
retrieved by Fisher from the
wreck of the *Atocha* which
sank in 1622.

President Harry Truman's
former winter home in Key
West, just beyond the western
end of Southard Street, is
known as the **Little White
House**. It was remodelled for
him after his first visit to Key
West in 1946, and it was here,
two years later, that he held he
famous conference of joint
chiefs-of-staff to plan the
unification of the armed forces.
Restored to its earlier
appearance, the house opened
to the public in 1991.

A recent Key West attraction is
**Fort Zachary Taylor Historic
Site**. Fort Taylor, a pre-civil
war relic, recalls a time when
Union troops occupied the
island. Though the remainder
of Florida was a firm part of the
Confederacy, the Union flag
flew over this fort and
prevented a takeover by the
rebels. Part of the recreational
section includes a pleasant
beachfront. Another of the
island's fortifications, **East
Martello Tower** now houses an
historical museum and art
gallery.

A variety of sportfishing is
available almost any time of the
year in Key West – from off
Atlantic Ocean reefs and the
Gulf of Mexico; from Gulfstream
big-game angling; to backwater
angling. A day's deep-sea
fishing from the Key West boat
docks is a memorable
experience. Less ambitious
anglers will find their challenge
in the natural coral reefs and
among the many shipwrecks in
Key West waters. Younger
fishermen can enjoy simply
casting a line at minimal cost.
Since the island city of Key

One of the notable sights on the tiny isle: Key West's White Church

West is a mere 3½ by 1 mile 5.6 by 1.6km) in size, getting around is simple. You don't even need a car to see most of t, but if you would rather not walk, take an Old Town Trolley our which offers transport to and from hotels and gives narrated tours of the historic andmarks, including the old Navy docks, with a climb up Solaris Hill, the city highest point. You can leave the tour at any stop and rejoin it later. A popular alternative is the Conch Tour Train comprising small, open canopied cars.

Accommodation

There are lodges, b&bs and hotels throughout the Keys and the tourist office will help you with bookings. **Cheeca Lodge**, **The Reach**, **Marriotts Casa Marina Resort** and **Pier House** are all recommended. Many Key West b&bs are in charming old houses, but they are also very expensive. Camping areas are prolific in the Lower Keys.

Children

Any children who are water babies, or can throw a fishing line, will love the Keys. Dress is casual and evening activities finish early. Most enjoyment is found in John Pennekamp State Park (Key Largo), Islamorada and Key West.

Restaurants

The most chic restaurants are in Key West, but there is no shortage of places to eat good seafood: shrimp, of course, and red snapper, tiny grunts and stone crabs. Look for oyster bars and menus which feature conch and clams. A number of restaurants favour Cuban and Bahamian cuisine but other ethnic restaurants have recently been established.

Well-known restaurants in Key West include **Louie's** **Backyard**, 700 Waddell Avenue (tel: (305) 294 1061) and **Harbor Lights**, Garrison Bight Causeway (tel: (305) 292 0219).

Shopping

Most of the shops are in Key West, where there are street stalls, smart boutiques and much more. Many are to be found along Duval Street, and around Mallory Square which has a market. Local souvenir shops sell naturally sculpted driftwood, coconut products and straw items.

A tranquil sunset setting for fishing in the Florida Keys

LEE ISLAND COAST

The Lee Island Coast is an area of Florida not widely known by tourists. Many of its islands are still undisturbed or barely inhabited; some are only accessible by boat. Their names alone are evocative: Sanibel, Captiva, Estero, Pine, Cayo Costa, Punta Blanca, Cayo Pelau, Buck and Devilfish Keys, Johnson Shoals and Chino Island. This is a coast with a Caribbean aura, offering pristine secluded beaches and marvellous sunsets, but within easy reach of the 'City of Palms', Fort Myers.

Although the weather here is good all year round, the best value for money is between Easter and mid-December, which Lee County calls its 'Secret Season'. Here in southwest Florida, with its hundreds of offshore barrier islands, there is less development, but accommodation is plentiful and reasonably priced.

This is the perfect location for boaters; there are around 25 marinas in the area, where you can rent a solitary motor boat or become part of a fully-fledged sailing flotilla. Conditions are always good, and the boating byways meeting here include the Intracoastal Waterway, the Okeechobee Waterway and the Gulf of Mexico.

Beachcombers are likely to find all manner of shells strewn along the scenic beaches; there are over 400 species, including tulipshells, oliveshells, paper figs and junonia. This section of the state also lays claim to some fine nature sanctuaries covering thousands of acres. Among the best are the **J N 'Ding' Darling National Wildlife Refuge**, the Sanibel-Captiva Conservation Foundation, the Lee County Nature Center, **Carl E Johnson Park** (see below), Matanzas Pass Wilderness Preserve, Mound Key and Cayo Costa State Island Preserve.

WHAT TO SEE

◆
BLACK ISLAND
If for no other reason, come here for a delightful picnic at Lover's Key in **Carl E Johnson Park**. Visitors are driven by 'tram' across scenic mangrove islands to reach the picturesque beach. There is a snack bar, canoes for rent and nature trails through the park. Black Island lies just south of Estero Island.

◆
BONITA BEACH
Occupying the southern boundary of the Lee Island Coast, Bonita Beach (between Fort Myers Beach and Bonita Springs) is one of the west coast's best beaches. There are shops and restaurants here (many with waterfront views) as well as some cottage-style and condominium accommodation. On the sporting side, there's greyhound racing at the Naples/Fort Myers Kennel Club in Bonita Springs between October and early August, and Imperial River, one of Bonita Springs' most precious natural resources, offers the best canoeing in the area. You could

take the children to **Golf Safari** in Bonita Beach Road, where waterfalls and tropical gardens are the setting for an 18-hole miniature golf course – or to **Everglades Wonder Gardens** in Bonita Springs (one of the state's first attractions) for native and exotic wildlife including Big Joe, a 1,000-lb (450-kg) crocodile, and some playful Everglades river otters.

CABBAGE ISLAND

Just the place for the island dreamer who doesn't want to be completely deserted. Life is quiet here but the company is usually interesting at the tiny inn which used to be part of the estate of mystery writer Mary Roberts Rinehart. The inn only has six guest rooms but it does have a very popular dining room papered with autographed dollar bills – worth around $10,000 to date if it were all taken down! It has become a custom for first time visitors to follow the tradition. **Cabbage Key** is built on top of an ancient Caloosa Indian shell mound – one of the highest elevations in the southwest. There are nature trails to explore, a water tower to climb for a panoramic view of Pine Island Sound, and a marina. Find these at Channel Marker 60 in the Intracoastal Waterway, north of Captiva; accessible only be boat.

◆

CAPE CORAL

A relaxing place to stay and enjoy the outdoor life with 14 recreational parks. There are fishing opportunities in **Four Freedoms Park** and several others, as well as playgrounds and picnic facilities. **Ecology Park** features a nature trail and observation tower and **Lake Kennedy** has a beach. Cape Coral is a mainland coastal community bordering the Intracoastal Waterway, looking across to Pine Island.

CAPTIVA ISLAND

It was to this tiny island that pirate José Gaspar, who plundered his way through the locality, sent his captives. This is a Florida version of Tahiti: lush, encircled by white sand and mangroves, and colourful with hibiscus.
There are two major resorts. At **South Seas Plantation**, guests can opt for a hotel room, villa or guest cottage; choose from several places to dine; play golf or tennis, or take sailing lessons at the marina, or join a fishing or shelling charter.
Shelling is the main attraction on Captiva. Simply walk along **Blind Pass Beach** and you can see shells spilled on to the shore with each fresh wave. Miniscule but colourful coquinas are the most common; you might find a sand dollar (a bleached flat white shell) or rare black shark's teeth.
Other activities include watersports and cycling and there are around a dozen restaurants on Captiva. Six miles (10km) long, this is a sister island to **Sanibel** (see pages 41–2), to which it is connected. An extensive

wetland tract with nature trails lies between the two islands, which are easily reached from the mainland via a 1-mile (1.6-km) toll causeway.

◆
CAYO COSTA
Cayo Costa is the region's largest undeveloped barrier island, and is only accessible by boat. It is being developed into a state park – the Florida Department of Natural Resources maintains primitive cabins in the northern section, near Johnson Shoals – but most visitors come for the day to fish, bathe, hunt for shells or venture inland to admire the native flora. Many shorebirds nest here in spring and in summer, and sea turtles lay their eggs on the beaches.

◆
ESTERO ISLAND
One of the most popular and lively destinations in the area, this is the site of Fort Myers Beach. Because there are no dangerous undertows or riptides, this is a particularly safe beach for children. Compared with neighbouring islands, Estero's social life is quite racy. All the hotels are by the beach; all the restaurants serve fresh seafood, including red snapper and grouper. You can catch your own – from the numerous piers and docks, or by joining a charter boat from one of the marinas in search of tarpon. Watersports include jet skis, catamarans and parasailing. Family amusements include two unusual golf courses: **Jungle Golf**, a mini-

course surrounded by larger-than-life African animals and **Smugglers Cove**, set amid pirates and shipwrecks (both on the San Carlos Road).

◆◆◆
FORT MYERS
This city is the hub of activity for the region, with shopping malls, restaurants and nightclubs. Thomas Alva Edison predicted that Fort Myers would become a popular metropolis when he built a winter home here in the 1880s. His friend and business associate, Henry Ford, built his winter home alongside Edison's and today both houses are open as the **Edison Winter Home** and the **Ford Winter Home**. The tropical gardens are a major feature; Edison planted flowers and trees here for experimental purposes. He studied species like hibiscus, Rose of China, Moreton Bay figs and vine trees, in the hope of

Phonograph horns in the Edison Museum form an unusual bouquet

yielding some beneficial product. His experiments with golden rod on the estate actually did produce a new strain of plants which grew to 14 feet (4m) and were 12 per cent rubber. Edison also started planting McGregor Boulevard (which passes the house) with stately royal palms. The city took over the project in 1917, and the Avenue of Palms now stretches for 15 miles (24km). Edison's first view of Fort Myers was on a trip down the Caloosahatchee River. Certainly the climate influenced his decision to stay, but he also had his eye on the wild bamboo growing along the river banks, as he was using bamboo filaments in his new electric lights.

The chemical laboratory you see today is still lit by light bulbs Edison made in 1912. But the electric light was only one of over 1,300 inventions which he patented. A fascinating **museum** within the house documents many of these and displays early prototypes of phonographs, light bulbs, cinematic and telegraphic equipment, toasters, heaters, water softners, electric fans and many other remarkable objects, as well as personal momentoes.

The **Ford Home**, next door, is surprisingly modest and also includes a museum dedicated to the owner's achievements during his time there.

Fort Myers Historical Museum is a Spanish-style depot with displays on the Calusa Indians and local cattle ranchers. The museum also houses a scale model of Fort Myers at the turn of the century, a large glass collection and an early transportation display.

Visitors can take a self-guided tour around the restored hub of Fort Myers, which runs along First Street, with its old style shopping arcades and restaurants – maps are available from the downtown tourist centre.

Musicals, concerts and dance performances are frequently staged at the **Barbara B Mann Performing Arts Hall** on the campus of Edison Community College, adjoining a Gallery of Fine Art. Star shows are given at the planetarium at the **Nature Center of Lee County** on Ortiz Avenue.

The **Everglades Jungle Cruise**, from Fort Myers Yacht Basin, offers a choice of tropical island buffet, night time dinner cruise or excursions to Lake Okeechobee.

In North Fort Myers, **The Shell Factory** is a good place for buying gifts and souvenirs; shells, corals and other merchandise is spread over 70,000 square feet (6,500sq m) of space.

Some 15 miles (24km) south of the town is the **Koreshan State Historic Site**, the home from 1894 to 1908 of Cyrus Reed Teed ('Koresh') and a bizarre religious group who believed the earth was a hollow sphere. You can tour the house and grounds and learn more of their beliefs (note: there is no connection between these Koreshan and the infamous cult led by David Koresh who perished at Waco in 1993).

GASPARILLA ISLAND
This was the island where pirate José Gaspar buried his booty. Today **Boca Grande** has become a haven for the rich and famous. It was founded by the DuPont family in the late 1800s and now offers waterside accommodation, charming shops and restaurants. Visitors may amble on the beach here, admire the old lighthouse or cycle down shady Banyan Street. Most of all they come to fish, especially for the thrill of hooking tarpon.

◆
PINE ISLAND
Situated next to Gasparilla Island, this island is named for its towering pines, and is accessible by bridge. It has always been known for commercial fishing, and as yet it has no high rise hotels or tourist attractions. The charming small waterfront village of Bokeelia is a remnant of an older Florida. From here you can hire a boat and visit the more remote islands.

SANIBEL ISLAND
Along with her sister isle, **Captiva** (see pages 38–9), Sanibel is a popular vacation spot, often touted as 'Florida's Tahiti'. Sanibel is the easiest to reach and the most popular, with a happy balance between nature and modern development. The main thoroughfare is Periwinkle Way, a pretty road canopied by Australian pines. From the Sanibel Lighthouse, on the island's eastern tip, to Tarpon Bay Road, it is dotted with craft shops, boutiques and cosy restaurants. Works of the area's most successful artists can be purchased at **The Schoolhouse** and **Matsumoto Galleries**. Visitors stay mostly in resort hotels,and enjoy golf, tennis and cycling including tandems and fringed surreys. The most popular activity, however, is shelling – an obsession for

Luxurious properties have not spoiled the beauty of Sanibel Island

collecting exotic sea shells. This island's configuration makes it one of the world's three best shelling beaches, since the smooth and gentle slope of the gulf bottom allows even the most fragile shells to be brought in undamaged. Everyone here seems to be afflicted with the 'Sanibel stoop' as they bend low and hunch their backs in their search for Tiger's Eyes, Kitten Paws, Angel Wings and Ladies' Ears. If they can't be found on the beach, they can be bought in one of the innumerable shell stores. Before you begin your own shell collection make sure you know the regulations on the taking of live shells (see **Peace and Quiet**, pages 108–9). In the northern half of the island is the **J N 'Ding' Darling National Wildlife Refuge**, which can be visited by bicycle or car. From the 5-mile (8-km) roadway built on top of a dyke it is easy to spot heron, egrets, plovers and the ibis stalking the mud flats below. There are also walking and canoe trails from which osprey and brown and white pelicans can be spotted.

◆

USEPPA ISLAND

Well-heeled boaters and fishermen make up the Useppa Island Club, but visitors can also see the island (accessible only by boat) if they make a reservation to do so. The club house is a restored version of the original mansion which millionaire Barron G Collier built in the early 1900s. Collier's original pink

promenade still exists, leading from the island's north end to the inn.

Pirate José Gaspar was one of the first to discover Useppa, which he inhabited from time to time, though his main headquarters were at Sanibel.

Accommodation

Visitors can stay at the **Sonesta Sanibel Harbour Resort and Spa** (tel: (813) 466 4000). On Sanibel, recommendations include the **Sanibel Beach Club** (tel: (813) 472 3382); **Ramada Inn Beach & Tennis Resort** (tel: (813) 472 4123); **Sanibel Island Hilton Inn** (tel: (813) 472 3181); **Shell Island Beach Club** (tel: (813) 472 4497); and **Signal Inn Beach & Racquetball Club** (tel: (813) 472 4690). At Fort Myers Beach is the **Outrigger Beach Resort** (tel: (813) 463 3131). There are many reasonably priced motels here and in Fort Myers itself.

Children

The islands are fine for the very young who are happy with paddling and sand castles, but there are not many special activities. The best family attractions are the **Shell Factory** and the **Everglades Wonder Garden**.

Restaurants

Fresh fish is the ideal order at local restaurants on the larger islands such as Estero, but Fort Myers has the widest choice.

Shopping

The biggest choice of shops is in Fort Myers and Fort Myers Beach.

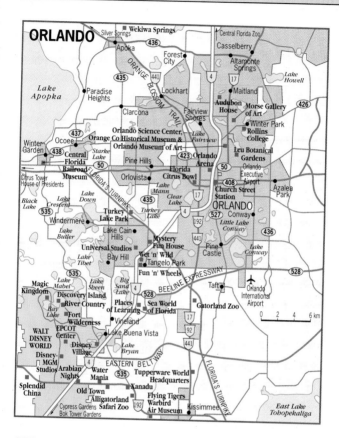

ORLANDO & VICINITY

Think of the Orlando area and one feature is likely to spring to mind: theme parks. A host of these parks are scattered in and around a city which in the past 50 or so years has grown from a small trading post on a cattle range into an impressive, landscaped modern city with its own international airport. This middle state region occupies the spread between Ocala National Forest and Lake Okeechobee.

Originally cattle country, it became better known for its citrus orchards in the 1800s. Today's visitors will find both rodeos and orange groves, not to mention horse farms. Although most tourists come here for the man-made attractions, Orlando and vicinity boast innumerable natural attributes. Central

Florida is not called 'Lake Country' for nothing; there are literally thousands of lakes, and two of the state's largest rivers, the Peace and Kissimmee, flow through here. There may not be a coastline or splendid beaches, but there are numerous opportunities for watersports.

Some of the fun and fantasy parks pre-date World War II, but it was Walt Disney's decision to purchase a site in the mid 1960s that sparked the development whose results can be seen today. Hotels and motels mushroomed; transport facilities were vastly improved; restaurants opened in their hundreds; small towns became vacation centres. Orlando itself is not the only holiday base; Kissimmee, for example, is a resort area in its own right within equal proximity to major places of interest, as well as to the airport.

WHAT TO SEE IN AND AROUND ORLANDO

◆
ALLIGATORLAND SAFARI ZOO
4580 West Irlo Bronson Memorial Highway, Kissimmee/St Cloud
A chance to see Florida's most famous wildlife along a mile-long (1.6km) boardwalk trail. There are over 2,000 alligators in the park, ranging from babies to 1,500-pounders (680kg).

◆
APOPKA
A useful base for **Wekiwa Springs State Park** where you can camp, picnic, swim or rent a canoe.

◆◆
ARABIAN NIGHTS
Kissimmee
This attraction was developed at a cost of $20 million and is one of Orlando's most popular dinner shows. Located in a stadium designed as an Arabian palace, it can seat 1,000 visitors who dine whilst watching the show. The entertainment features talented horses and includes famous Lippizaners, Quarter Horses and American Saddlebreds. They even recreate *Ben Hur's* chariot race.

◆
CENTRAL FLORIDA RAILROAD MUSEUM
Winter Garden
The Tavares & Gulf Railroad Depot, built in 1913, has been restored to exact detail. There are some 3,000 pieces of railway history on display here. Open Sunday afternoon only.

◆◆
CENTRAL FLORIDA ZOO
Sanford
This 110-acre (45-hectare) park features a small but important collection of some 250 birds and animals, including monkeys, hippos, otters and several members of the cat family. A petting corner with rides (weekends only) keeps young children happy. Take Interstate 4 (exit 52).

Costumed Southern Belles are a trademark of Cypress Gardens

◆
CLERMONT

This is the heart of citrus country. A 200-foot (60-m) high **Citrus Tower** has been specially erected so that visitors may get a bird's-eye view of the groves. Take the Citrus Grove Tram Tour through a 10-acre (4-hectare) grove. Just a little further along on North Highway in Clermont is the **House of Presidents** where wax figures of America's past leaders, through to President Clinton, are on display.

◆◆◆
CYPRESS GARDENS

near Winter Haven

One of Florida's showpieces, which can truly claim to appeal to all the family. The park covers 223 acres (90 hectares) these days, though when it started in the 1930s it comprised only 16 acres (6.5 hectares) and its main attraction was the exotic botanical gardens. There are still 16 acres (6.5 hectares) of flower-lined pathways with more than 8,000 varieties of plants from 75 different countries on display at various times of the year. One highlight is the 1,500-year-old giant bald cypress tree, representing the native cypress plants which gave the gardens their name. Another special feature is the annual chrysanthemum festival in November. It's colourful at any time of year, though.

In the **Animal Forest** zoological park there is plenty to see: an Exotic Bird Revue, a daily alligator handling demonstration, an oceanic and wading bird exhibit, and a special corner where young animals may be petted. Young and old alike enjoy this area with its pygmy goats, baby camels and huge Aldabra tortoises. The Island in the Sky ride is a great observation point; a revolving platform on a huge crane-like arm, which hauls its way up from ground level to over 150 feet (46m). Cypress Gardens is best known for its good old-fashioned Southern style, personified by the Southern Belles – pretty young ladies who adorn the grounds in their traditional hooped antebellum dresses. It is equally renowned, however, for its skilful and exciting waterski revues.

And there's lots more. The latest attraction is Wings of Wonder, a huge conservatory housing over 1,000 free-flying butterflies, along with exotic waterfowl and even a family of iguanas. Allow a whole day to see everything in comfort.

GATORLAND ZOO
Yes, this does mean alligators, and there are over 5,000 of them. The zoo is a commercial alligator farm and research facility, as well as being a tourist attraction. If you've always wanted to hold an alligator, this is the place to visit, and don't worry – they're either non-biting babies or carefully muzzled. You could also take one of the nature trails through a cypress swamp for a close look at Florida wildlife.
This zoo was the setting for the alligator scenes in *Indiana Jones and the Temple of Doom*.

◆

HARRY P LEU GARDENS
Lake Rowena, North Orlando
These relaxing gardens feature all kinds of exotic plants; the rose garden and orchid house are of particular interest. A turn-of-the-century farmhouse is now a museum.

◆◆

KISSIMMEE
This is Orlando's tourist dormitory town, with plentiful accommodation at low prices. Only a 25-minute drive from the airport and within easy reach of the theme parks. It was first settled in 1878; in 1880, Broadway, now one of its main avenues, was still covered in Bermuda grass, had boardwalks on either side and a railroad down the middle. It used to be a cattle-ranching area and rodeos are still held every Friday night at the Kissimmee Sports Arena.
Today the area attracts thousands of visitors. Its main feature is **Old Town**, a speciality shopping and eating area patterned after a turn-of-the-century Florida town, where you can visit a wood-carving museum, ride an antique carousel or take a horse-drawn surrey.
There are several other attractions, including **Xanadu** (a futuristic home), **Medieval Times/Medieval Life**, a themed dinner show and exhibition, plus a good waterpark, **Water Mania** (page 53) and the **Splendid China** theme park (page 49).

LAKE WALES
This resort, which is situated on Lake Kissimmee, supplies all the lakeside recreation you could wish for, with fishing, boating and nature trails. It is best known however, for **Bok Tower Gardens**, a peaceful retreat created in the early 1900s. The 225-foot (78-m) tower houses a 57-bell carillon which gives daily recitals at 3 pm.

ORLANDO
There's much more to Orlando than Walt Disney World.

Cinderella Castle towers over Fantasyland, a favourite for small children in Disney's Magic Kingdom

International Drive, a bustling neon-lit artery, chock-a-block with restaurants, shops and hotels is the real heart of the town. Along here too are 'fun houses', go-kart tracks and themed mini-golf courses plus branches of **Ripley's Believe It or Not!** and **Mel Fisher's World of Treasure** (see **Key West,** page 34).

Downtown Orlando features a historic district which is undergoing restoration and is best known for **Church Street Station**, an excellent night-time entertainment and shopping complex.
If you want to learn how Orlando developed, head out to peaceful Loch Haven Park, 4 miles (6.5km) northeast of Downtown. Here you'll find the **Orange County Historical Museum**, the **Orlando Museum of Art**, and

the combined **Orlando Science Center** and **John Young Planetarium**. All are worth a visit (closed Monday and weekend mornings).

◆◆◆
SEA WORLD✓

7007 Sea World Drive, Orlando
This is the most visited marine life park in the world. Sea World is dedicated to marine research and educating the public by means of the most entertaining shows and best possible displays of marine life. Top of the bill is Shamu, the 6,000-lb (2,700-kg) killer whale whose shows, together with her baby, Namu, are almost legendary. Terrors of the Deep is a walk through the world of sharks, barracudas and other predators, while dolphins, manatees, penguins and sealions provide more appealing company. There are shows throughout the day and you'll need to spend at least a day here.

Even killer whales become star performers in Sea World's entertaining displays

◆◆◆
SILVER SPRINGS
5656 N E Florida Boulevard, near Ocala
This multi-themed nature park enjoys an idyllic setting. At its heart is the largest artesian limestone spring in the world, pumping crystal-clear water into the Silver River. The highlight here is a glass-bottom boat ride along the river, spotting creatures both indigenous (alligators, anhinga birds, racoons) and introduced (monkeys, giraffes, gazelles and other African species). There are two different rides, a jeep safari and lots more, so allow a full day.

Children will want to try out the **Wild Waters** waterpark next door.

◆◆
SPLENDID CHINA
US 192, Kissimmee
Imagine 5,000 years of Chinese history, exquisitely crafted by Chinese artisans into miniature model village detail, and you have an idea of Florida's latest theme park. There are over 60 splendid monuments, including the Great Wall, made from over 6 million 2-inch (5cm) long bricks, the 9,999-room Imperial Palace of the Forbidden City and the fabled Terracotta Army. There's a stunning film to see and plenty of authentic Chinese street entertainment and demonstrations.

For many visitors, the restaurants alone are worth the trip here.

◆◆◆
UNIVERSAL STUDIOS ✓

Universal pioneered the concept of the film studio as a theme park with their Hollywood operation from 1966 onwards and in 1990 opened studios in Orlando alongside Disney-MGM. The format of the park is very much in the Disney mould, with 'animatronic' robots, special cinematic and simulator effects and rides all designed to take you into the world of motion pictures.

There are behind-the-scenes tours and audience presentations so that by the time you leave you have a very good insight as to how movies are made.

King of the rides is undoubtedly Back to the Future, a mind-blowing chase (based on the film *Back to the Future II*) which takes current simulator technology to its limits. Other popular rides and shows are based on *Jaws*, *King Kong*, *Ghostbusters*, *ET*, *Earthquake*, Alfred Hitchcock films and Hanna-Barbera cartoons. With *Jurassic Park* coming soon it's a large and formidable roll call (the studios are much bigger than those at Disney-MGM) and you need two days to see it all in comfort.

◆◆◆
WALT DISNEY WORLD ✓

Now synonymous with Florida, Walt Disney World is the world's leading tourist attraction. It occupies a 43-square mile (111 sq km) site the size of a large city and comprises three major theme parks, two water parks, a nature island, a night-time entertainment complex, a shopping village, a campground and numerous hotel resorts. The Magic Kingdom is the most famous of all with its Disney characters bringing back to life all those memories of childhood. EPCOT combines educational and cosmopolitan elements while Disney-MGM Studios has the most adult appeal. Each park is different but all feature themed rides or 'adventures' which involve cinematic special effects including Circlevision (the screens surround you) and life-like animated models known as 'animatronics'.

Your introduction to the **Magic Kingdom** is Main Street USA, an idealised re-creation of turn-of-the-century small town America. Off here there are four main sections – Adventureland, Frontierland, Fantasyland and Tomorrowland, containing over 45 rides and 'adventures'. Fantasyland is geared to very young children but also includes the spectacular Legend of the Lion King live theatre production, Tomorrowland is the world of the future while other lands' themes are quite general.

The following are the showpiece attractions. Space Mountain, a hair-raising roller coaster in the dark, is something of a theme park legend. Splash Mountain is a thrill ride on water, reaching speeds of up to 40 mph (64 kph) and culminating in a five-storey plunge. Pirates of the Caribbean is a much gentler boat ride through a series of sets depicting a port being sacked by pirates and features Disney animatronics at their best. The Haunted Mansion isn't at all frightening but the special effects are first class. Big Thunder Mountain Railroad is a runaway train roller coaster speeding its way through old mining tunnels, and past lots of amusing animatronics.

American Journeys is a wonderful Circlevision film which takes you coast to coast by plane, helicopter, boat and train.

Jungle Cruise is a gentle ten-minute cruise through waterfalls, jungles, the Nile Valley and the African Veldt, encountering animatronic animals. Daily events include a carnival procession.

EPCOT is an acronym for Experimental Prototype Community of Tomorrow and was conceived by Walt Disney as a real-life community. Sadly, it proved impractical, though the Future World section of EPCOT still retains one of the original objectives of 'showing off the latest US technologies and the imagination of free enterprise'. Here the emphasis is less on thrills and more on learning.

The highlights of Future World are as follows: Universe of Energy, where films and an ingenious moving theatre ride take you through 'the forces that fuel our lives'. Wonders of Life includes an exciting

*Taking the plunge on Splash
Mountain's log flume ride*

simulator thrill-ride, an
animatronic show plus a
humorous and sensitive movie
(*The Making of Me*). Listen to
the Land (in The Land Pavilion)
is a cruise through various
world climes to see how
agriculture may look in the
future. The Living Seas
features the world's largest
man-made salt-water tank with
over 80 species of tropical fish
and mammals. Finally,
curiosity alone may demand a
ride into the landmark silver
'golf ball' that is the symbol of
EPCOT and hosts Spaceship
Earth.

The other half of EPCOT is
World Showcase. Here eleven
countries have done a
remarkable job of trans-
forming a few square yards of
Florida into the buildings,
sights, sounds, smells and
tastes of their home land.
Each pavilion has its own
architectural showpiece (from
a Mayan pyramid to the Eiffel
Tower), shops and at least
one restaurant demonstrating
the culinary excellence of the
host country. Norway, Mexico,
China, United States, France
and Canada also feature a
ride and/or a Circlevision film.
The best pavilions are Mexico,
China, Japan, Morocco,
France and Canada. The end
of every day at EPCOT is
celebrated in the most
breathtaking fashion by
Illuminations, a pyrotechnic
extravaganza of lights, lasers,
fountains and music.
Disney-MGM Studios has

Hollywood Boulevard instead
of Main Street USA in this
magic kingdom for film lovers
and once you have seen one of
the other Disney theme parks
you will know what to expect in
terms of animatronics, rides
and special effects. However,
Disney-MGM is also a live
working studio and the
excellent Backstage Studio
Tour gives a splendid insight
into what goes on behind the
scenes. To see how cartoons
of all kinds are created take
the Animation Tour. The other
highlights are Star Tours, the
Twilight Zone of Terror and the
Indiana Jones Epic Stunt
Spectacular. The former is a
thrilling space flight simulator,
which has all the excitment of
actually being inside the
cockpit of a Star Wars craft
during a hair-raising,
hyperspeed adventure. The
Twilight Zone is an unnerving
journey through a haunted
hotel before a heart-stopping
ride in a lift that is 'going down'

with indecent haste. The Stunt Spectacular is a live production on a huge outdoor stage with Indy (actually a look-alike) re-enacting some of the most heart-stopping scenes from his blockbuster movies. Other attractions include audience participation shows demonstrating sound effects and the craft of television production, plus Muppets attractions and a walk-through adventure based on *Honey I Shrunk the Kids!* Largest of all Disney's ride-through attractions is The Great Movie Ride, which reproduces some of the greatest moments in film history. During the summer and holiday times the Sorcery in the Sky fireworks show ends the day in style at Disney-MGM.

Pleasure Island is a vibrant evening entertainment complex comprising seven nightspots, the Empress Lilly steamboat, various restaurants, shops and a movie theatre. One admission ticket gets you into all clubs, which open at 7pm.

Both the Comedy Warehouse and The Adventurers Club are comedy venues. The first is fairly conventional, though no less funny for that, the second is in the style of a 1930s gentlemen's Travellers' Club where animal heads on the wall talk and you are ushered into the club's 'private library' to hear tall tales. The Neon Armadillo features live country and blue-grass music, while the Rock & Roll Beach Club hosts live bands playing dance oldies and recent rock music. Mannequins is a high-energy state-of-the-art disco with a touch of Disney magic and 8 Traxs bring back those heady 1970s days of *Saturday Night Fever*. The latest offering is the Pleasure

Welcome to the movies – a behind-the-scenes adventure in cinematic style

Island Jazz Company with live jazz and rhythm 'n' blues.
River County is an idyllic Huckleberry Finn-style swimmin' hole, with rope swings, slides and flumes. The whole area is beautifully landscaped, complete with a lovely white-sand beach which is also good for swimming.
Typhoon Lagoon is four times the size of River County and is probably the world's most innovative water theme park, combining the Disney eye for fantasy detail and immaculate landscaping. Thrilling water slides and rapids rides spew out from an 85-foot (26-m) high mountain and you can catch a 6-foot (1.8m) wave on the amazing inland body surfing lagoon. There is a Caribbean reef where you can snorkel among exotic fish and here too is a perfect beach. Queues for the slides can be long and the best time to visit is Monday, Tuesday, Friday or Sunday morning.
Discovery Island, a beautifully landscaped zoological island, is the perfect retreat when you have had a surfeit of crowds, queues, animationics and thrill rides. Nature trails and walk-through aviaries feature parrots, monkeys, flamingoes, alligators and giant tortoises in natural habitats.

Swim at the Wet 'n' Wild water park

◆◆
WATER MANIA
West Highway 192, Kissimmee
One way to keep cool on a hot day! Water Mania features a wave pool and several thrilling water slides. The park includes an activity area for children, a pleasant sandy beach and picnic spot.

◆◆◆
WET 'N' WILD
International Drive, Orlando
This is the biggest and best water park in Florida, and one of the finest in the world. Every conceivable method of high-speed hydro-sliding is explored here from the terrifying six-storey sheer drop of Der Stuka to the Black Hole, an equally exhilarating turning and twisting ride in the dark aboard an inner tube. New rides are being continually introduced and include the Surge, the longest water ride in Florida at nearly 1,800 feet (600m), but there are lots of gentle rides too and

the park caters for youngsters of all ages.

Accommodation

You are spoilt for choice here. The number of motels, hotels, resorts and self-catering units available increases each year. If Walt Disney World is your top priority then consider staying on site at one of the many Disney resorts.

Disney World Resort Hotels include:

Disney Inn, located near Palm and Magnolia championship golf courses. In addition to luxury accommodation, there are putting greens, driving ranges, lighted tennis courts plus swimming pool.

Contemporary Resort, situated on Bay Lake, adjacent to the Magic Kingdom, this 15-storey A-frame tower hotel, with north and south accommodation wings, is very popular. The Magic Kingdom monorail arrives in its lobby and there's a good view from its Top of the World supper club.

Polynesian Village Resort, in the Polynesian Village section conveys a South Seas atmosphere. Guest rooms are located in 'long houses'; the swimming pool has its own waterfall and is surrounded by tropical foliage; *luaus* (Polynesian feasts) are held nightly.

Grand Floridian Resort, 900-room luxury, turn-of-the-century style hotel next to the Seven Seas Lagoon.

Caribbean Beach Resort, southeast of EPCOT, with over 2,000 rooms, six restaurants and seven pools.

On and around Highway 192, try **Park Inn International**, an all-suite hotel; **Ramada Resort Maingate East at the Parkway**; **Howard Johnson Fountain Park Plaza**; and **Wilson World Hotel** are all in the Kissimmee/St Cloud area. There are many budget motels, too.

Restaurants

There is a multitude of restaurants to suit all pockets and tastes, from fast food to gourmet spreads. A variety of eating places exists at most of the theme parks. Magic Kingdom options are limited, but many of the EPCOT restaurants are outstanding. Book through a central reservation system as you enter EPCOT to avoid disappointment. Orlando is also known for its dinner shows, casual fun nights with mass-catered food to a specific theme while being entertained: **Arabian Nights**, **Asian Adventure**, **Capone's**, **King Henry's Feast**, **Medieval Times**, etc. Other variations on this theme are the murder-mystery or the dinner theatre show (*eg* the **Plantation Dinner Theater**).

Shopping

Gift shops are to be found at all the theme park attractions, in the heart of Orlando, such as at the **Church Street Station Exchange**, the **Mercado Mediterranean Village** on International Drive, and in Kissimmee's **Old Town**.

'St Pete' Beach, a resort connected to the mainland by causeway

THE PINELLAS

When Spanish explorers sailed round Florida's west coast in the early 1500's they saw an area which they called *punta pinal*, or 'point of pines'. From that name comes today's word Pinellas, which refers to a string of eight resort communities along 128 miles (206km) of white sand.

Altogether, this 'Suncoast' playground takes up 265 square miles (680sq km) from Tarpon Springs in the north to St Petersburg in the south. The 'Suncoast' title is promotional – but records maintain that the area enjoys an average of 361 days of sunshine a year.

As a resort destination for overseas visitors, the Pinellas is relatively new, though for Americans it was discovered years ago, once Henry Plant had extended his railroad and steamship routes into Tampa in the 1880s and opened the glamorous Tampa Bay Hotel in 1891. Nowadays, Tampa is an international gateway served by many airlines including US Air, British Airways, Delta and TWA, and accommodation ranges from the sleek and sophisticated to the more affordable seaside motels.

The Pinellas tends to be less expensive than the more familiar eastern 'Gold Coast' (Miami and the Palm Beaches), yet it is nearer to the attractions of Orlando and boasts some first-class sights of its own. The region has evolved into a casual, relaxed and reasonably priced part of Florida.

Watersports are available here all the year round – from simple swimming to the more invigorating jet skiing and parasailing. The area is well noted for fishing, particularly off shore, deep sea; the tarpon appear in late spring/early summer. Some of the resort properties specialise in tennis or golf, with beautiful court locations and scenic courses. For those who would rather watch than participate, there is also American football, baseball, dog racing and *jai alai* (see **Hialeah Park**, page 20). The emphasis in the Pinellas is on relaxation, but there is a lively cultural life here, too, with orchestral productions, ballet and arts festivals. St Petersburg's Bayfront Center and Clearwater's Richard Baumgardner Center for the Performing Arts both offer a particularly wide range of activities. Some of the communities here have a European air – Dunedin, for example, where the Scots settled in 1870 and still celebrate the Highland Games in March or April; or the Greek-influenced sponge-fishing town of Tarpon Springs.

WHAT TO SEE IN AND AROUND THE PINELLAS

CALADESI ISLAND
Its name means 'beautiful bayou', and this state park may only be reached by boat (private or ferry service from Clearwater, Clearwater Beach and nearby Honeymoon Island). Yucca and palms add their own grace to

Ivory sands at Clearwater Beach, part of the city of Clearwater

this peaceful isle, which covers 1,4000 acres (567 hectares), 3 miles (5km) offshore from Dunedin Beach. It is a refuge for wading birds, but there are food and picnic facilities, a children's playground and 2 miles (3km) of white sand. This is an ideal place for swimming, shelling or fishing, skin and scuba diving and nature study – a 3-mile (5-km) trail winds through the interior. For a view of the whole island, there is a 60-foot (18-m) observation tower.

CLEARWATER
Visitors here will soon understand Clearwater's nickname – "The

dolphins (8 to 16-year-olds can attend marine biology class here in summer; classes free, but there is a charge to enter). **Ruth Eckerd Hall** on McMullen-Booth Road is part of the performing arts complex, presenting not only music but dance, fun and fantasy, with regular art exhibitions in its gallery. The Florida Orchestra is based here and the Florida Opera gives performances during the year.

Next to the St Petersburg-Clearwater airport, the **Florida Military Aviation Museum** features restored aircraft and aviation artefacts dating from World War II. The nearby **Boatyard Village** is a re-created late 19th-century fishing village, with shops, restaurants and a theatre. By way of contrast to the man-made, take a look at **Moccasin Lake Nature Park**, east of US19, where many examples of the area's native plant and animal species are to be found. A 1-mile (1.6 km) nature trail winds through the 50-acre (20-hectare) park and there are wildlife exhibits and displays at the Interpretive Center.

Sparkling City'. The Gulf waters do sparkle in the sun, and watersports are given high priority. This is the seat of Pinellas County, both a growing city and fashionable coastal community with a 2-mile (3-km) expanse of popular white sandy beach. Here you can fish from **Pier 60**, which stretches out into the Gulf, rent a boat from the marina or take a cruise. Several are available, including picnic cruises on a pirate ship, and one which offers on-board dinner dances. Events include the Kahlua Cup International Yacht races in November.

The **Clearwater Marine Science Center**, a research facility on Windward Passage, displays marine life (live and models), including baby sea turtles and

◆
DUNEDIN

This resort, which adjoins Clearwater, was founded by Scots in 1870 and their influence is evident in the architecture, the street names and, of course, the festivities. In fact, the settlement used to be known as Jonesboro, until two enterprising merchants petitioned the government for a post office to increase business for their store. They requested the name 'Dunedin', a Gaelic term meaning 'peaceful rest'. Peaceful it is, except perhaps during the Highland Games in April, when the bagpipes come out along with dancing and drumming, and booths selling Scottish wares and food. Before the railway, Dunedin was one of the chief ports between Cedar Key and Key West for the shipping of fruit and vegetables. A visit is recommended to the **Dunedin Historical Museum** on Main Street, which was a station for the Orange Belt Railroad system, dating from 1889. Drawings and relics from the Scottish community's past are displayed here (open Tuesday, Thursday and Saturday mornings, 2 October to 31 May). Among other registered buildings are the Andrews Memorial Chapel and the J O Douglas House. The **Fine Arts and Cultural Center** on Michigan Avenue features some good exhibits and an arts and crafts shop. Free admission.

◆◆
HOLIDAY ISLES

This is the collective name given to several beaches in the Pinellas: Indian Shores, Indian Rocks Beach, Belleair Beach, Redington Shores, North Redington Shores and Redington Beach. Novice sailors may rent boats from any of these beaches, which offer 10 miles (16km) of sand and Florida's longest fishing pier, at Indian Rocks.
Indian Rocks Beach is the site of **Hamlin's Landing**, a

Victorian waterfront shopping and dining complex alongside the Intracoastal Waterway. Closeby, at Indian Shores is the **Suncoast Seabird Sanctuary**, Dr Ralph Heath's hospital for birds on an acre (0.4 hectare) plot near the beach. Dr Heath was 25 when he saw a cormorant struggling with a broken wing in the middle of a highway. He rescued the bird and treated it, the news spread, and soon other sufferers were arriving. What was once a temporary casualty department has become permanent with its own operating theatre and intensive care unit. Over 40 species reside here, including the largest collection of brown pelicans in captivity. Injured birds are frequently brought to this sanctuary, and those that recover enough to fly again are released. Dr Heath is usually on hand to answer questions from visitors. Among the stories he tells is one of a pelican with a broken wing which dragged itself for a mile (1.6km) to reach the sanctuary gate; and another of two crippled pelicans who produced the first offspring to be hatched and raised in captivity. There is no entrance charge here, but donations are happily accepted since it is a non-profit making organisation – and visitors are encouraged to 'adopt a bird'.

◆
HONEYMOON ISLAND

Like neighbouring Caladesi Island, this is one of the few undisturbed barrier islands in the Gulf of Mexico, but Honeymoon does have access to the mainland via the Dunedin Causeway. The island got its name when a developer built fifty thatched honeymoon bungalows here. Now a state park, with a rare stand of original pine, long beaches and mangrove swamps, it provides for outdoor activities such as swimming, shelling, fishing, picnics and nature study.

◆◆
LARGO

There are two reasons for a visit here. The **Heritage Park & Museum** on 125th Street North comprises a fascinating collection of restored homes and buildings in a pine wood setting. The actual museum forms the centrepiece, holding examples of pioneer life at the turn of the century. Most notable is the house of a prosperous Victorian family, a tiny honeymoon cottage and a Cracker-style log cabin typical

of early pioneers. There are often features craft demonstrations. Admission free (closed Mondays).

On the same street, **Suncoast Botanical Gardens** feature a variety of cacti and local flora including eucalyptus trees growing up to 85feet (26m) tall, plus palms, crepe myrtle and other plants. Admission free.

◆◆
MADEIRA BEACH

This popular resort community at the centre of the Pinellas has in John's Pass one of the best fishing inlets in the state, whether for big game or easy angling. Visitors can rent a charter boat and head for the deep seas or inland fishing on Boca Ciega Bay – or merely throw a line from the docks. **John's Pass Village & Boardwalk**, designed as a traditional fishing village of

Tradition by design: John's Pass fishing village, Madeira Beach

ramshackle wooden structures with tin roofs, house, shops, restaurants and galleries. It is also home to a large commercial and charter fishing fleet. Many events and festivals take place here during the year and a paddle-wheel riverboat offers lunch and sightseeing cruises along the Intracoastal Waterway. The beach itself, north of John's Pass, covers some 2½ miles (4km) of fine sand.

SAFETY HARBOR

This place was well known to the Indians and the Spanish for its healing mineral springs. One mile (1.6km) north of the village centre, a museum at **Philippe Park** showcases local artists' work, and a history museum displays local artefacts. The park, which overlooks Tampa Bay, was named after Count Odet Philippe, a French aristocrat, who settled the site in the 1800s. This is the oldest continually cultivated orange grove in the state.

ST PETE BEACH

Although this is classified as part of St Petersburg, it is an island resort in itself, connected to the mainland with a 7½-mile (12-km) strand of sands bordered by hotels, beach bars and restaurants. It has its own marina, charter boat fishing and sightseeing cruise boat; its own fishing jetties and sports facilities; its own discos and piano bars. Its most recent addition is the **Gulf Beaches Historical Museum**.

ST PETERSBURG

Occupying the southern tip of the peninsula, St Petersburg is the most cosmopolitan of all the Pinella communities, combining city appeal with nearby 'St Pete' Beach (see opposite). There is a great deal of the pseudo-Spanish style which became so fashionable during the Florida land boom but St Petersburg is essentially 'modern' in appearance.

John Williams from Detroit founded St Petersburg in 1876 on the site of his farm. Having given up farming he turned to town planning, engaging the assistance of exiled Russian nobleman Peter Demens, who brought his Orange Belt Railroad into the new town in 1888. Legend has it that they tossed a coin to see who would choose the new town's name; Demens won and named it after his birthplace.

Good weather made this a winter retreat, especially for the elderly, but these days St Petersburg is a lively, sunny resort for all ages, sometimes referred to as the 'sailing capital of the south'. Many a prestigious racing event and regatta takes place annually here and it is easy for anyone to rent a variety of boats, or take a lunch or dinner cruise on Tampa Bay. The recently renovated **Pier**, which extends for half a mile (0.8km) into Tampa Bay, is a major landmark. The inverted pyramid structure at the end of it contains shops, an aquarium, a marine exhibit, an observation deck and places to eat. There is a choice or beaches near by –

*Beaches and sailing have boosted
St Petersburg's growth as a resort*

either downtown or 30 minutes
or so away, on the Gulf, but St
Petersburg offers more than
beaches. Athletic, cultural and
other entertaining events are
frequently held at the **Bayfront
Center. Derby Lane**, on Gandy
Boulevard, features greyhound
racing between January and
May (not Sunday) – visitors can
eat at the clubhouse

overlooking the track, and a
mini television on each table
gives closer race scrutiny.
Ballroom dancing still takes
place at the **Coliseum**, on
Fourth Avenue, on its 13,000
square feet (1,200sq m) maple
floor.

At the **Haas Museum**, on Second
Avenue, restored homes include
Lowe House built in 1850, Grace
Turner House, an old barber
shop, blacksmith's and railroad
depot. Open afternoons,

Thursday to Sunday. Still on Second Avenue, at number 335, the **St Petersburg Museum of History** features thousands of pioneer artefacts and pictures as well as collections of shells, coins, dolls and chinaware. The museum can be reached by a complimentary shuttle car from the pier. The **Museum of Fine Arts** nearby, on Beach Drive North, is noted for its collection of French Impressionist paintings. It also has a good collection of European, American, pre-Columbian and Far Eastern art. Permanent period rooms feature antiques and historical furnishings. One of the highlights here is the brilliantly displayed collection of Steuben crystal. Guided tours are available. Closed Monday. Special presentations are made between September and May in the **Planetarium** at St Petersburg Junior College Science Building. This sky theatre is under a large domed ceiling with scheduled performances September to May.

Just around the corner from here, on Second Street, is the **Florida International Museum**, hosting major cultural exhibitions from around the world.

Art lovers visiting St Petersburg should pay a visit to the **Salvador Dali Museum** on Third Street South – the world's largest single collection of Dali works under one roof; so large that works are rotated regularly. The collection includes 93 oils, 100 watercolours and drawings, along with nearly 1,300 graphics, sculptures and objets d'art.

There are signs of revival in the Tarpon Springs sponge industry

Love him or hate him, do take a free guided tour to learn about his brilliant precision, *trompe l'oeil* and double-imaging techniques. You'll never look at a Dali work in the same way again. Closed Monday mornings. Just across the street is **Great Explorations**, a great place for children who enjoy hands-on experiments in both arts and science subjects.

St Petersburg appeals to nature lovers too. **Sunken Gardens** is a very popular attraction on Fourth Street North, which has more than 50,000 tropical plants and flowers in bloom all the year round. A walk-through aviary features tropical birds and there are thousands of rare orchids in the Orchid Arbor. At the **Boyd Hill Nature Trail** on

native palms growing in the scenic section of Northshore Park on the famous waterfront.

◆◆
TARPON SPRINGS

The most northerly of the Pinellas coast communities, at the point where the Anclote River widens into bayous on its way to the Gulf, Tarpon Springs was first founded in 1876. The name stems from the fact that the first settlers thought tarpon spawned in the spring's bayous, though nowadays mullet are generally to be found.

Around 1905, Greek sponge fishermen moved here from Key West, convinced that the Gulf of Mexico held rich and sizeable sponge beds which they would be able to reach with their new improved diving equipment. They were right, and more and more Greek divers followed, bringing their customs and traditions with them.

In the 1940s marine bacteria destroyed the sponges and the men took other jobs or moved away. But recently it seems that sponges have become prolific again; the problem now is persuading young people into the diving business, which involves many hours at sea. Tarpon Springs is still very Greek however, and stores on its docks are filled with sponges in every shape and form. You might note that size does not necessarily indicate quality, and that various species are suited to various duties from cleaning the body to cleaning the car. Most of the activity here revolves around Dodecanese

Country Club Way South, there are six trails which lead through 216 acres (87 hectares) of natural beauty. The wildlife is fascinating and guided tours are available. **Fort DeSoto Park**, accessible by the Pinellas Byway off Interstate 275, south of St Petersburg Beach, was built during the Spanish American War and is located on Mullet Key, the largest of five islands which make up this unique country park. Fort DeSoto was built in 1898 to protect Tampa Bay, but the islands' history dates back before Ponce De León's arrival in the 16th century. Today, the park consists of 900 unspoilt acres (364 hectares) with 7 miles (11km) of beaches, two fishing piers, picnic and camping area. The **Kopsick Palm Aboretum** on North Shore Drive and Tenth Avenue features a range of

1920s chic: the impressive Don CeSar pink hotel

Boulevard and the **Sponge Docks**, where there are gift shops, Greek nightclubs and tavernas. **Spongeorama** uses diaramas and film to depict the history of the sponge industry; the museum is free, but a charge is made for the film. Tours of the village leave from here. It is also worth visiting **St Nicholas Greek Orthodox Cathedral** on North Pinellas Avenue, a replica of St Sophia's in Istanbul and the focal point of the Blessing of the Fleet during Epiphany. George Innes, the 19th-century American landscape painter, had a house and studio overlooking Spring Bayou, where both he and his son worked. The largest single collection of George Jr's work is to be seen in the **Universalist Church**, in Read Street, Tarpon Springs. Tarpon Springs' own Gulf beach, Sunset, is reached just a short drive along the causeway.

◆
TREASURE ISLAND
Located south of John's Pass, Treasure Island is a Pinellas resort with 4 miles (6km) of white sands – indeed, some of the broadest stretches anywhere along the Suncoast. A publicity stunt in the early 1900s created the name, and the area was formed with the merging of four communities in 1955. It still has three sub divisions: Isle of Capri, Isle of Palms and Paradise Island. Watersports are an obvious attraction: sailboats, paddleboats and windsurf boards may be rented from the southern end of the island; but there is also a golf course, and, at the Paradise Island tennis complex, 21 courts which are open for public use. Pirate Day, on 4 July, is the big celebration here, when a mock pirate invasion is staged to capture a treasure chest.

Accommodation
There are hundreds of motels with thousands of rooms in the Pinellas as well as hotels and holiday flats. Two of the most historic hostelries are the

Belleview Mido Resort and the **Don CeSar Beach Resort**. The former is a sprawling Victorian structure overlooking Clearwater harbour. It was opened in the 1890s and has recently undergone a multi-million dollar renovation. The towering 'pink castle' of the Don CeSar Beach Resort on St Petersburg Beach, opened in the 1920s. The guest list at both has always been something of a Who's Who. Also among the best are the **Sheraton Sand Key Resort**, on Clearwater Beach, with its private beach, water sports, floodlit tennis courts and Sky Lounge entertainment, and the **Breckenridge Resort Hotel**, at St Petersburg Beach, whose rooms all feature kitchenettes and whose poolside bar has live entertainment. **Innisbrook Resort**, at Tarpon Springs, is popular with the golfing fraternity, providing 36 holes of championship golf, as well as a tennis and racquetball centre and a spa and health club.

Children

The Pinellas beaches and the range of watersports are enough to keep younger members of the family happily occupied without further distractions, but the region has several other attractions for children. The world-famous African-themed **Busch Gardens** in Tampa is only a 30-minute to 1-hour drive away (see pages 69–71) and Orlando's popular theme parks can be reached in two hours.

Restaurants

There are well over 1,500 restaurants along this coastline, ranging from the elegant candlelit diner-for-two variety to barefoot casual, and even including moonlight dinner cruises. Seafood is a speciality and is always fresh and plentiful; try the elegant **Wine Cellar** at North Redington Beach or for fun, **Crabbie Bill's** at Indian Rock's Beach. The **Friendly Fisherman** at Madeira Beach is simple but good. It's also worth sampling the barbecued ribs with pit-baked beans and garlic toast at the **Hickory Smoke House** in St Petersburg. There is a distinctly British touch at the **Harp and Thistle Pub**, at St Petersburg Beach, right down to the draught Guinness and Bass. For romantic dining with a difference, try the Mississippi-style sternwheeler cruise from Hamlin's Landing or dinner with entertainment at the **Showboat Dinner Theater** in Clearwater or the **Royal Palm Dinner Theater** in North Redington Beach; Tarpon Springs has a number of Greek tavernas.

Shopping

The Pinellas boasts around 80 shopping centres and malls, though the waterfront village boutiques are the most tempting. Few can resist buying at least one sponge in Tarpon Springs. Visit **Boatyard Village** in a cove on Tampa Bay for its boutiques and galleries; try the speciality shops at **Hamlin's Landing** along the Intracoastal Waterway at Indian Rocks Beach; or **John's Pass Village** at Madeira Beach.

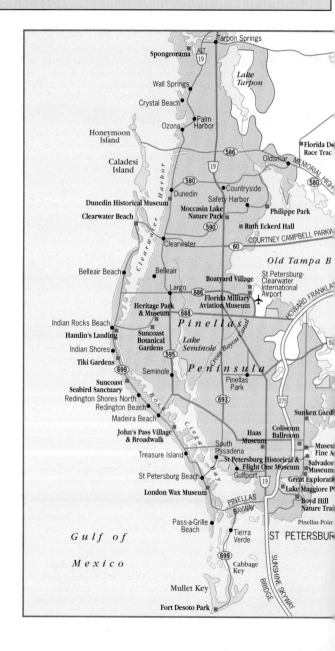

Tarpon Springs

Spongeorama

ALT 19

Lake Tarpon

Wall Springs

Crystal Beach

Ozona • Palm Harbor

Honeymoon Island

586

19

Oldsmar

■ Florida De Race Trac

MEMORIAL HIGH

580

Caladesi Island

580

Countryside

Dunedin

Safety Harbor

Dunedin Historical Museum

Moccasin Lake Nature Park

Clearwater Beach

590

Philippe Park

■ **Ruth Eckerd Hall**

Clearwater

60

COURTNEY CAMPBELL PARKW

Old Tampa B

St Petersburg-Clearwater International Airport

Belleair Beach

Belleair

Boatyard Village

HOWARD FRANKL

Largo

686

Florida Military Aviation Museum

Heritage Park & Museum

688

92

P i n e l l a s

Indian Rocks Beach

Hamlin's Landing

Suncoast Botanical Gardens

Lake Seminole

Indian Shores •

Tiki Gardens

595

P e n i n s u l a

699

Seminole

Pinellas Park

Suncoast Seabird Sanctuary

Redington Shores North

Redington Beach

693

275

Sunken Gard

Madeira Beach

John's Pass Village & Broadwalk

Haas Museum

Coliseum Ballroom

Treasure Island •

South Pasadena

Museu Fine A

St Petersburg Historical & Flight One Museum

Salvador Museum

St Petersburg Beach

Gulfport

19

Great Exploratio

Lake Maggiore P

London Wax Museum

PINELLAS BAYWAY

Boyd Hill Nature Tra

Pinellas Poin

Pass-a-Grille Beach

Tierra Verde

ST PETERSBUR

Gulf of

699

Cabbage Key

SUNSHINE SKYWAY

Mexico

Mullet Key

BRIDGE

Fort Desoto Park

Clearwater Harbor

Clear Bay

Cross Bayou Canal

Roc

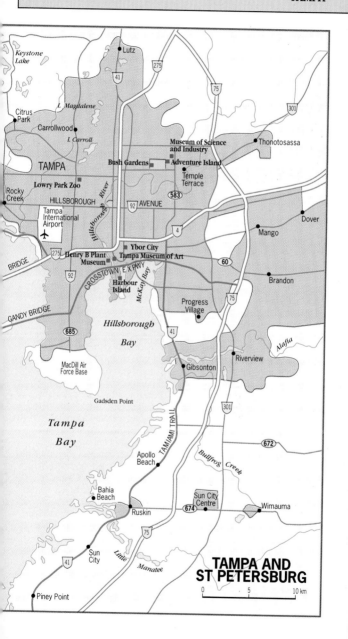

TAMPA AND
ST PETERSBURG

TAMPA

The quiet Indian fishing village of Tampa, on the bay, known as Espiritu Santo, was discovered by Europeans in the early 16th century. By 1580 Tampa had acquired its present-day name, though whether this means the 'town near the bay' or more poetically 'fire sticks' is a matter of debate. By 1823 Tampa was established as an army settlement and changed its name to Fort Brooke, but as troops left the army to join the Confederacy its population dwindled to insignificance. Towards the end of the century the fortunes of the town (by now known as Tampa again) were revived in typical Florida fashion by two visionary entrepreneurs. The first was Vicente Martinez Ybor who in 1885 successfully transplanted the Key West Cuban cigar-making industry to Tampa. Former Key West workers and new immigrants came to roll cigars by hand in the new area of Ybor (pronounced Ee-bore) City and until the 1930s, when an efficient cigar-rolling machine was invented elsewhere, Tampa was the cigar capital of the world. By 1891, however, Henry B Plant, the railroad tycoon, had opened his eastern railway line all the way to Tampa and had created the palatial Tampa Bay Hotel. Visitors flocked in and Tampa became a gateway to the pleasures of Florida's east coast.

Today Tampa is the regional business centre, it boasts the country's seventh largest port, and phosphate mining, brewing and cigars still make it an important industrial centre. Tampa's most famous tourist attraction, Busch Gardens actually developed from humble origins as a modest brewery hospitality centre. Today it is the biggest tourist honeypot on the west coast.

Although Tampa has never become the resort that Henry B Plant may have once envisaged it draws in many tourists and during the last decade or so has developed new attractions to persuade them that there is more to the city than just Busch Gardens. Harbour Island, a shopping and entertainment complex in the same vein as Miami's Bayside, and the re-vamped Ybor City, where you can learn all about cigars and still see them rolled by hand, are the most obvious examples. Besides these there are the sort of high-quality museums that you would associate with a city of this stature plus first-class performing arts and sporting venues. The arts have been boosted by the Tampa Performing Arts Center, a three-theatre complex on the banks of the Hillsborough River. Sports lovers may be interested to learn that the Cincinnati Reds and other major baseball league teams carry out their spring training here and the autumn sees American football with the Tampa Bay Buccaneers and the Hall of Fame Bowl. Being

The 'Python' slithers along a hair-raising route at Busch Gardens

by the Bay, there are many opportunities for watersports, including motor boating, wind surfing or taking out a hobie car (small catamaran). As for the festivals, Tampa is at its liveliest during the annual revelry of the Gasparilla Festival in January/February and when it hosts the State Fair in February. During early March there's a Strawberry Fest in neighbouring Plant City and in Brandon, a Balloon Festival each October.

WHAT TO SEE IN AND AROUND TAMPA

◆◆◆ BUSCH GARDENS ✓

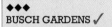

Busch Boulevard and 40th Street
This 300-acre (121-hectare) African-themed park appeals to all ages, featuring thrill rides, live entertainment, animal shows and exhibits, shops, restaurants and games. Over 3,300 animals are at home in eight distinctly themed sections, such as the 'Congo'

and the Tropical Bird Gardens. Busch Gardens is 6 miles (10km) from downtown Tampa, and 1¼ hours' drive from Orlando. One entrance fee pays for all the park's activities. Today it is recognised as one of America's top zoos, has the most fearsome roller coasters in the state and is also reknowned for its water rides. Simulator rides have also recently been added.

Visitors enter the park via the Morocco section where artisans can be watched at work, and their wares examined. Designed to resemble a typical walled Moroccan city, with elaborate tile work, snake charmers and belly dancers, this section offers several shows; some, such as a spectacular ice show, are performed in the 1,200-seat Moroccan Palace Theatre. The next section is Nairobi, home to the animal nursery, the Nairobi Train Station, a petting zoo and Nocturnal Mountain – a display of night creatures in a 'night time' setting so that visitors may view their natural behaviour. Busch Gardens is noted for conservation. For example, four out of five Asian elephants born in captivity in North America have been born here, and there is a special nursery for newborn animals, with large viewing windows for park guests. Part of this sector of the park is a one-acre (0.4-hectare) elephant exhibit, a simulated version of the animals' natural habitat amid rock formations, greenery, waterfalls and a swimming hole. Elephant rides are available. 'Serengeti Plain' may be viewed from the monorail sky ride, by steam locomotive, or simply by walking along the west promenade. Over 500 head of African game roam freely on this veldt-like plain including impala, giraffes and zebras. Elephants, Nile crocodiles, dromedaries, flamingos and ostriches also live here. 'Timbuktu' features thrilling rides – looping roller coasters, a boat swing ride, Sandstorm thrill ride and the Carousel Caravan with camels and Arabian steeds. This section also features dolphin shows, a shopping bazaar, an electronic games arcade and a German themed dining and entertainment complex.

Past this quarter lies the 'Congo',

Several hours are needed to sample all of Busch Gardens' activities

one of the most action-packed sections of the park. This is where you can take a white water raft ride, the Monstrous Mamba or the Swinging Vines. A special feature here is Claw Island, displaying rare white tigers in a natural habitat. In lively Stanleyville, visitors can browse through African crafts, watch a variety show, take a log flume ride or the tamer cruise boat ride, and observe free flying birds. Watch the antics of the cockatoos in the Bird Gardens Theatre, see Eagle Canyon, where flightless golden and American bald eagles reside, and take the children to the play area (parents could complete their time at Busch at the brewery, where

complimentary beer is served). A recently added attraction is Crown Colony, an *Out of Africa* themed area with plantation house and colonial restaurant. Adjacent to the park, **Adventure Island** is a separate, 22-acre (9-hectare) water-themed park. Here one can take the Rambling Bayou, a leisurely float trip down a winding river – the 76-foot (23-m) high Tampa Typhoon free fall slide, the Gulf Scream speed slide, the Everglides toboggan slide or the Barratuba inner tube slide. Flume slides and pools are also available.

LOWRY PARK ZOO
7530 North Boulevard
Attractions in this recently renovated and extended zoo include the Asian Domain, Primate World, and a Manatee and Aquatic Center. The shaded boardwalks lead you through the animals' near-natural habitats. Guided tours are available.

MUSEUMS
Art and cultural exhibits frequently change at the **Tampa Museum of Art** on North Ashley Drive, which also holds one of the finest collections of Greek and Roman antiquities in the southeast United States (closed Mondays). Across the Hillsborough River, the administrative offices of the University of Tampa now occupy Henry Plant's exotic Tampa Bay Hotel, but the **Henry B Plant Museum**, set up in one wing, exhibits his sumptuous collection of Victorian arts and furniture (closed Monday). Near Busch Gardens, the **Museum of Science**

and Industry (**MOSI**) is Florida's largest science centre featuring over 200 hands-on displays, plus a planetarium.

◆◆
YBOR CITY

This is Tampa's historic Latin Quarter, with wrought-iron balconies, plazas and arcades, and sidewalk cafés. Tampa flourished after Vicente Martinez Ybor moved his cigar-rolling factory here from Key West in 1886. Cubans were hired to work in the factories, hundreds of them rolling cigars by hand. The old factory has since become **Ybor Square**, with shops and theatres, but its story is told at the **Ybor City State Museum**, and you can still buy a hand-rolled cigar here (see also **Shopping**).

Accommodation

Large hotels and self-catering holiday flats are plentiful. All the big chain names are here, including Hyatt Regency, Marriott, Holiday Inn and Hilton.

Children

The treat for youngsters is Tampa's own theme park, **Busch Gardens** or the **Lowry Park Zoo**.

Restaurants

The wide range includes those offering first class seafood and those with a view of the Bay. Ybor City offers Cuban/Spanish cuisine and strong black coffee. Another popular eating area is The Market on Harbour Island where you'll find speciality shops, dining and dancing venues all leading to the Waterwalk. Harbour Island is reached via two bridges or the elevated People Mover shuttle.

Shopping

A good choice of boutiques can be found on **Harbour Island**. At **Ybor Square**, refurbished factory buildings enclose shops selling a wide range of antiques, imports, arts and collectables. Other shopping centres include the **Tampa Bay Center**, **University Square Mall**, **West Shore Plaza**, **Belz Factory Outlet** and **Old Hyde Park Village**.

The Kapok Tree restaurant gardens near Tampa

WHAT TO SEE ELSEWHERE IN FLORIDA

AMELIA ISLAND
Northeast coast
This island lies at the entrance to the St Mary's River, the most southerly of what Floridians refer to as the Golden Isles. It's a combination of lush oak glades and palmetto with salt marsh and rolling sand dunes. In 1686 it was known as Santa Maria with a Spanish Mission at what is now Fernandina Beach. South Carolina's governor, James Moore, attacked the island with an English force and Indian allies in 1702, captured the post and destroyed the Mission, and there were so many subsequent attacks that by 1730 Amelia was all but deserted.

It acquired its present name in 1735 when General James Oglethorpe re-established a post here, naming it after English King George II's sister, Princess Amelia. When Florida was returned to Spain in 1783, a large tract of the island's land was given to Don Domingo Fernandez, including a village named Fernandina in his honour. It became the haunt of pirates and smugglers in the 19th century.

Fernandina Beach is today's main reason for a visit, a colourful old port with a restored historic district downtown where gas lamps light up Victorian homes and visitors are invited to bend an elbow over the hand carved antique bar of a 19th-century saloon. Guides offer walking tours of the historic district and the island's rich 400-year history is best explained at the **Amelia Island Museum of History** on South Third Street (closed Sunday).

Also of historic note is **Fort Clinch State Park**. Construction of the fort was begun in 1847, one in a chain built along the Atlantic coast, but was never completed. It was seized by Confederate troops in 1861 and abandoned in 1862 to Union troops, who used it as a prison. Nowadays, it is open daily as a museum. On the first weekend of each month it features a living history interpretation in which the year is 1864 and the garrison soldiers are going about their daily duties.

APALACHICOLA
Northwest coast
This town lies at the mouth of the Apalachicola River and is almost completely surrounded by water. It produces around 90 per cent of the state's oysters from thousands of acres of oyster beds.

In town, the major point of interest is the **John Gorrie State Museum**, named after a resident doctor who invented an ice-making machine in the 1840s which was to be the forerunner of the air conditioner and compression refrigerator. Gorrie invented his machine to cool the rooms of patients suffering from yellow fever but, although he patented the device in 1851,

ELSEWHERE IN FLORIDA

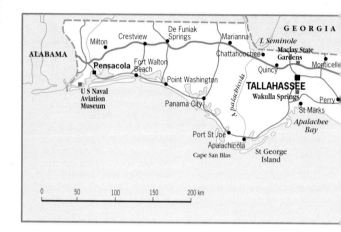

could not raise the money to develop it commercially. He died in 1855 without ever having gained recognition for his work.

Within the Apalachicola National Forest is **Fort Gadsden State Historic Site**, once a fort held by Indians and runaway slaves against US forces. In the park you can picnic, fish, boat or take the nature trail. Also within the forest's boundaries is the **St Mark's National Wildlife Refuge**, a paradise for ornithologists. **Apalachicola National Forest** comprises more than half a million acres (0.2 million hectares), spreading west from Tallahassee to the river. Wildlife is plentiful and there are excellent spots to camp, fish or swim.

◆◆
BOCA RATON
Southeast Florida
The name may mean 'mouth of the rat' but this Gold Coast resort for the privileged is lively and attractive. The Spanish gave the site its name because of the many sharp and jagged rocks, like teeth, just below the surface at this point of the coast. These, in combination with the domed thatched Indian huts they saw near the beach, led to the nickname 'rats' nests'.

Eccentric architect Addison Mizner envisioned Boca Raton as his dream city in the 1920s – an American Venice, since at the time a grand canal was etched down the main thoroughfare to the sea (nowadays El Camino Real). The town was a shipping centre for winter fruit and vegetables, until Mizner decided to decorate the canal with ornamental landings and Venetian style bridges, and, in keeping with this theme, transport visitors by electric gondola.

Mizner's dream was never really fulfilled – the toppling of Florida's land boom saw to

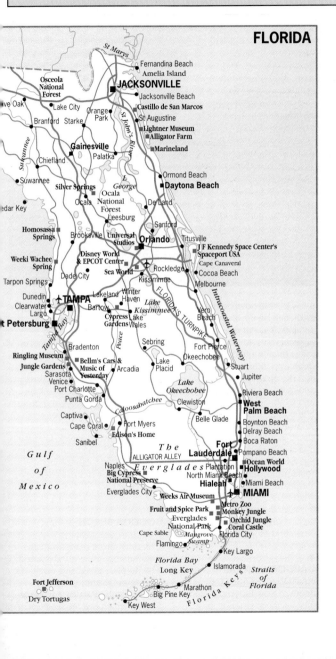

that – but the hotel he designed in 1925 to be the 'flossiest hotel around', has survived. The original was named the Cloister Inn, a hostelry that has since been expanded, embellished and developed into the glossy and giant Boca Raton Hotel and Club. Since then, too, golf courses, condominiums, villas and holiday homes, shopping complexes and marinas have all sprouted in the vicinity. Speciality restaurants and Spanish-styled shops, dinner theatres and winter polo games, not to mention the beach itself, all help to give Boca Raton a plush and monied air.

◆
CAPE CANAVERAL NATIONAL SEASHORE

South of New Smyrna Beach, this seashore extends for 25

Cape Canaveral National Seashore, a haven for coastal wildlife

miles (40km). At the southern end, Playalinda Beach is good for swimming and surfing. The central position has remained undeveloped, a place to look for giant loggerhead and green turtles among the dunes and sea oats. In the summer, the turtles crawl ashore to lay their eggs. Climb the boardwalk to Turtle Mound, where for centuries the Indians piled up shells.

◆
COCOA BEACH

Central east coast

An oceanfront resort with an expanse of white sand fronted by hotels, restaurants and bars. At the southern end of the beach is the **Patrick Air Force Base**, which has a collection of missiles on display to passers-by (no admission). The **Brevard Art Center and Museum** is renowned for its high-quality touring exhibitions (closed Monday). The community of Cocoa itself is across the Indian River on the Intracoastal Waterway, connecting with the Atlantic.

◆

DADE CITY

A small but charming community south of Bushnell on US301, Dade City has a southern air with its azalea blooms and moss-draped oaks and camphor trees. Closeby is the **Dade Battlefield State Historic Park**, where an 1835 Indian ambush sparked off the Second Seminole War. The 80-acre (32-hectare) park is a memorial to Major Francis Dade and his men who died here. The Park includes nature trails and picnic spots.

◆

DANIA BEACH

Southeast coast
A 2-mile (3-km) palm-shaded strip of public beach not far from Miami. It used to be known as the 'Antique Centre of the South' and there are still 'finds' to be made, but few bargains. Just to the north on the A1A, the **John U Lloyd Beach State Recreation Area** is a partially-developed barrier island, providing visitors with places to fish, swim and boat.

◆

DAYTONA BEACH

Central east coast
Best known for its International Speedway and that perennial

main event in February, the Daytona 500. Other big races include the Pepsi 400 each July, and motorcycle races every March and October. The first permanent settlement was made in 1870 by an Ohio man named 'Day'. Daytona became associated with motor racing because its beach – 500 feet (150m) wide, with 23 miles (37km) of hard white sand smoothed by incoming tides – proved ideal for the sport. The **Birthplace of Speed Museum**, Ormond Beach, celebrates the early days of car racing here and exhibits include a 1922 Model-T. (Open afternoons Tuesday to Saturday.) To get more up to date with the Daytona racing scene visit the **World Center of Racing** at the International Speedway Stadium and the nearby **Klassix Auto Museum**. Motor racing apart, Daytona is a cheap 'n' cheerful holiday resort with fairs and amusements centred around the **Pier** and the **Boardwalk**. For the best view, climb to the top of the 176-foot (54-m) Space Needle. The **Museum of Arts and Sciences** (closed Mondays) includes history displays and a planetarium, and for relaxation there are sightseeing cruises to Ponce de León Inlet, its historic lighthouse and nearby islands.

◆

DEERFIELD BEACH

Located just south of Boca Raton and bordering the Everglades region of the Loxahatchee National Wildlife

Refuge, where airboat rides and fishing are available, Deerfield Beach's highlight is **Island Park** – a tiny island in the Intracoastal Waterway, accessible only by boat. Today this is a great spot for fishing and bird watching, but it used to be notorious as the hideout of Chicago gangster Al Capone.

Of interest in the town is the restored **Old Schoolhouse**, housing memorabilia from the 1920s, and **Pioneer House**, built of pine and a typical example of local architecture.

◆

DE LAND

Central east Florida

Founded by and named after Henry Deland in 1876, this is a good base for nature lovers heading for nearby wilderness areas. An attractive town with oak-lined streets, De Land hosts many events during the year, the most popular of which is the annual Artists Sidewalk Art Festival, which, in March, attracts participants from all over the country.

The main site of interest lies 6 miles (10km) north: **De León Springs**, discovered by Ponce de Leon in 1513. The springs form a subterranean stream pouring out a staggering 19 million US gallons (427,324 litres) of water everyday. They are surrounded by a well-shaded area rich in birdlife, Indian burial grounds and recreational facilities. Boat tours of St John's River are available not far from De Land and a ferry provides transport to nearby Hontoon Island.

◆

DELRAY BEACH

The main attraction on this attractive low-key resort near Fort Lauderdale is **Morikami Park**, with its ½-mile (0.8km) self-guided nature trail and **Museum of Japanese Culture** (closed Monday), donated to the county by the last survivor of the Yamato colony of Japanese pineapple farmers.

◆◆◆

THE EVERGLADES

Most of Florida's southern tip belongs to the **Everglades**, comprising well over a million acres (0.4 million hectares) of marshland and sawgrass ruled by wildlife and for the most part left untouched. Indeed, it was never explored at all until the middle of the 19th century, when soldiers were sent in search of the remaining Seminoles, and attempts to reclaim the swamp were first made in 1903. There are several ways to enjoy the Everglades, but remember that the area is vast; don't expect to see more than a small section. Sightseeing excursions are made here from Florida's main vacation centres but visitors travelling independently can pick up a free map and information at the Visitor Center at the main entrance. For drivers' convenience, there is a road through the heart of the park, stopping at Flamingo. Stop once in a while and take to the boardwalks – but don't leave them; the Everglades remain a true wilderness and any alligators you see are not the

*The anhinga, or 'snake-bird',
keeps watch in the Everglades*

Disney kind! Hiking enthusiasts may certainly reach the centre of the park on foot, but perhaps the most enjoyable way of seeing this mangrove wilderness is by boat – canoe, airboat, or even houseboat. The area's wealth of bird and animal life, vegetation and waterways has made it one of the state's greatest national treasures. Six hundred varieties of fish, 300 species of birds, and 45 indigenous plant species are said to be found here. You should soon begin to recognise strangler figs, black racer snakes, wood storks, native orchids and gumbo-limbo trees, given time to explore. Hammocks – small islands of hardwood trees and shrubs – are scattered throughout the swamps, and dense thickets on the higher ground have probably been created by oaks, coco plums and custard apple trees, whilst the cypress is the most familiar vegetation on the lower ground. Visitors entering the protected National Park area at the northeast gate pass the Main Visitor Center. The road to the Royal Palm Visitor Center soon reaches Long Pine Key, where there is a 7-mile (11-km) nature trail, campsites and picnic areas. This base leads to the **Pa-Hay-Okee Overlook Observation Tower** and **Mahogany Hammock Trail**. Canoeists might try the 3-mile (5-km) Noble Hammock Trail but only the very experienced should attempt the **Wilderness Waterway**, the longest and most varied trail in the park. Even the less hardy can take advantage of the walking trails, which start from a ½ mile (0.8km) excursion to much longer distances. The **Anhinga Trail**, for instance, named after one of the native birds, stretches for just ½ mile (0.8km) along a raised boardwalk over the sawgrass, and the adjacent **Gumbo Limbo Trail** is the same length, winding through a

Elevated boardwalks offer close views of the Everglades' wildlife

hammock. The **Pineland Trail**, on the other hand, is 6½ miles (10km) long – but this is a good one for spotting some of the lovely orchids; and the **Pa-Hay-Okee Overlook Trail**, at 12½ miles (20km), does require stamina to complete. Many Everglades visitors head for the developed tourist section at **Flamingo** where, these days, there is accommodation, marine stores and a marina, though Flamingo was once an isolated fishing village accessible only by boat. The easy way to explore the surroundings is to take a tour boat from here passing Coot Bay, along the Buttonwood Canal and visiting Tarpon Creek before reaching Cape Sable where you can go ashore and take the **Wilderness Train** through mangrove forests and Snake Bight Trail.

Tram tours of the park start at Shark Valley and sightseeing tours by boat of the **Ten Thousand Islands** area start near Everglades City. These tangled islands of mangrove trees lie off the coast of Marco Island and the Everglades, and are formed from shell, driftwood and seaweed trapped in the mangrove roots. As the trees mature they topple into the water and take root again, so new islands are constantly being formed.

◆◆◆
FORT LAUDERDALE
Southeast coast
The 'Venice of America' has a touch of the Riviera, thanks to over 300 miles (483km) of

lagoons, canals and rivers, and miles of Atlantic beaches. Named after Major William Lauderdale, who built a fort here in 1838 during the Seminole Wars, Fort Lauderdale is a lively holiday centre. Even in its early days, tourists flocked here, maybe for its abundance of bars, gambling halls and brothels, for at one time it was considered a 'Sin City'. Rum runners brought in liquor by the crate from the Bahamas to keep the early tourists happy – among them a man named Bill Macoy, a rum runner who only carried the best brands of liquor – 'the real Macoy'. Tourists in the 1950s included droves of college students, who helped form the bright, youthful image of present day Fort Lauderdale. All the watersports ever devised are

Canals and inlets wind through Fort Lauderdale

available, including diving and snorkelling on the offshore reefs. Boating is probably the most popular, and facilities for chartering and sailing are excellent. A favourite way to take in the sights is by old fashioned riverboat – perhaps on a dinner cruise. Cruises aboard the **Jungle Queen** leave from the Bahia Mar Yachting Center on day or evening trips; in the evenings there is a barbecue and shrimp dinner, a vaudeville show and a singalong. In the daytime the cruise passes Millionaires' Row, and passengers can disembark at the Seminole Indian Village. **Paddlewheel Queen** cruises leave from one block south of Oakland Park Beach Bridge and also offer day or night sailings.

Fort Lauderdale is actually the hub of an intricate inland boating paradise that extends throughout Broward County. Boaters on this section of the Intracoastal Waterway tend to be dedicated to life on the water, but others can experience it in any size or type of vessel for any length of time. For a look at the more glamorous boats, go to Pier 66 marina or Bahia Mar.

Water makes an impact in other ways. Everyone will enjoy **Ocean World** at SE 17th Street Causeway, for example, where they will see sharks, sea lions, turtles, dolphin shows and an oceanarium featuring denizens of the deep. The **International Swimming Hall of Fame**, just behind the beach on Seabreeze Boulevard, not only hosts collegiate competitions

At anchor in Fort Lauderdale

but contains memorabilia from numerous countries.

Restaurants in the area serve some of the best seafood, supplied by the Atlantic Ocean and the nearby Gulf of Mexico. The choice is endless – as it is for hotels and shops. The traditional place to shop is Las Olas Boulevard, which extends for about 1½ miles (2·5km) from downtown.

State and regional parks are abundant, too. The closest is the 180-acre (72-hectare) **Hugh Taylor Birch State Park**, across the street from the ocean. In the **Historic District** the **King-Cromartie House**, furnished in turn-of-the-century style, may be toured (closed Monday).

The home of Fort Lauderdale's earliest white settlers is today a historical museum on Las Olas Boulevard – **Stranahan House** (open Wednesday, Friday and Saturday). But the place not to be missed is the **Museum of Discovery and Science and Blockbuster IMAX Theater**, an interactive museum complete with a giant special effects cinema screen – kids love it.

Art lovers should head for the **Museum of Art**, on East Las Olas Boulevard. Its permanent collection includes an important collection of Oceanic, West African, pre-Columbian and American Indian art (closed Monday). The best way to get to know the resort and its environs is to take the 18-mile (29-km) trip by the **Voyager Sightseeing Tram**, from South Seabreeze Boulevard, passing the residential areas and Port

Everglades. Another enjoyable way to explore is by water-taxi, on demand like a land taxi (tel: (305) 565 5507) from any safe dock, or with an excursion ticket for a day's cruising. Guided tours are also available.

FORT PIERCE

Situated on US1 and Florida 68 on the west side of the saltwater Indian River (in reality a lagoon). There are four public beaches and the **Fort Pierce Inlet State Recreation Area** which also has a beach. For a typical turn-of-the-century Floridian home and for Indian artefact displays, look into the **St Lucie County Historical Museum** on Seaway Drive (closed Monday).

FORT WALTON BEACH

Come to this lively playground of the northwest today and it's hard to believe that in 1910 black bears outnumbered people here! Luckily visitors are more likely to need a fishing rod than a rifle these days – its waters are teeming with fish. The pier stretches into the Gulf of Mexico for over 1,000 feet (305m) and fishing possibilities range from trolling to surf or freshwater. Yachting, is another prime sport – many regattas take place at Fort Walton Beach.

In the centre of the resort is the **Indian Temple Mound Museum**, a National Historic landmark depicting over 10,000 years of Gulf Coast living in the Choctawhatchee Bay area (closed Sunday). Northeast of

the city, Eglin Air Force Base offers tours which include its **US Air Force Armament Museum**; and across the bridge on Okaloosa Island is the **Gulfarium**, a marine attraction with dolphin and sea lion shows, a Living Sea exhibit and huge tanks where marine life may be studied at close quarters.

GAINESVILLE
North central Florida

This college town, located midway between the Atlantic and the Gulf, was named in 1853 to honour General Edmund Gaines, a leader in the Seminole Wars – an improvement on the former title of Hog Town! Much of the activity revolves around the campus of the **University of Florida**. The **University Gallery** is worth a look and nearby is the **Florida Museum of Natural History**. The best attractions, however, are the recently opened **Harn Museum of Art**, on SW 34th Street and Hull Road, which features American, African and pre-Columbian collections and the **Historic Thomas Center**, on NE 6th Avenue, a cultural centre featuring many exhibits and activities.

HOLLYWOOD

This beach resort is part of Broward County, close to Fort Lauderdale. Gift shops, cafés and restaurants all overlook the ocean along the Hollywood Beach boardwalk, but its biggest attraction for families is **Six Flags Atlantis**, a watery

The remains of Yulee Sugar Mill, built over one hundred years ago

theme park with a huge wave pool, slides, chutes and an 11-acre (4-hectare) lake. One entrance price pays for everything, including live entertainment and water ski shows.

Topeekeegee Yugnee Recreation Area is a lakeside park with canoes and paddleboats for hire, cycle trails and picnic sites; or sample the rides and water sport facilities in the newer **CB Smith Park**.

◆◆
HOMOSASSA SPRINGS
Central west coast

An ideal destination for the family, 2 miles (3km) from Homosassa itself (an Indian name meaning 'the place of pepper trees'). Here you can wander through botanical gardens, visit the underwater observatory or cruise along tropical jungle waterways in a pontoon boat. The springs pour out about 70,000 gallons (318,220 litres) every minute to form a natural aquarium and the highlight of a visit here is watching manatees in the wild. West of the springs, off US19, the **Yulee Sugar Mill Ruins** are on a state park, once part of a 5,000-acre (2,000-hectare) plantation, the property of David Yulee, Florida's first US senator. To the south of Homosassa is the **Chassahowitzka National Wildlife Refuge**.

JACKSONVILLE

The largest, most commercial town in the northeast is named after President Andrew Jackson and sits on the banks of St John's River. The **Riverwalk** is a pleasant promenade that lasts just over a mile (1.6km), bordered by shops and restaurants. **Jacksonville Landing** is a riverfront entertainment, dining and shopping complex connected to the town by elevated light railway. This was one of the state's earliest settlements for both the French and Spanish, who built forts near here. **Fort Caroline** has been reconstructed on its original 16th-century site, on Jacksonville Beach. Jacksonville has been a thriving town for well over a century. Seafarers filled its Bay Street bars, and their schooners filled its harbour in the 19th century, and it became a popular winter resort after 1863 when the first theatre and several large hotels opened. There are now several theatres in town, as well as a ballet troupe and

symphony orchestra with a year-round schedule. Downtown, the Friendship Park Fountain is illuminated at night and sprays water up to 120 feet (36m) high. Jacksonville has a number of interesting museums. The **Cummer Gallery of Art** is a fine arts museum with a good collection of paintings and sculptures (closed Monday). On Riverside Avenue a fine contemporary collection and some interesting porcelain are displayed at the **Jacksonville Art Museum** (closed Monday) on Boulevard Center Drive, while the **Museum of Science and History** on Museum Circle, has scientific and anthropological displays, several hands-on displays, a planetarium and aquarium. The city's **Zoo** at 8605 Zoo Road is also recommended; over 800 exotic and native animals can be seen in natural habitats in this 62-acre (25-hectare) park. They may be viewed from the elevated walkway or from the miniature railway. The **Anheuser-Busch Brewery**, on Busch Drive, admits parties free to see the brewing and bottling process and sample the end product. Jacksonville's holiday resort section is **Jacksonville Beach**, whose focal point is the beach pier and boardwalk.

JUPITER

Southeast coast

The best view of this small waterside community is from the **Jupiter Lighthouse**, a red brick landmark perched on a bluff, overlooking the Jupiter Inlet and the Gulf Stream. The

Wind and sand erosion has created these rock 'alligators' dotted with blow-holes on Jupiter Island's Blowing Rocks Preserve

lighthouse is still operational and also holds a small museum (open Sunday afternoons). The waterfront is good for restaurants. Restful places to visit for wildlife are located to the north of Jupiter: **Hobe Sound National Wildlife Refuge** is reached via US1 – sea turtles nest on the beach here and nature trails are marked for hikers. The nearby **Jonathan Dickinson State Park** is a departure point for river boat tours and has canoes, bicycles and cabins for rent.

◆◆◆
KENNEDY SPACE CENTER/SPACEPORT USA

Spaceport USA is a great day out for anyone who has ever wondered what it is like to be an astronaut or who would simply like to see all that incredible space hardware close up. Tours start at the Galaxy Center where the Rocket Park, a group of historic space rockets pointing proudly skywards, gets you in the right frame of mind. Inside the Center, the Gallery of Space Flight and various other exhibition areas give you a good introduction to the trials and tribulations of Space Age technology. Don't worry if it's all a little bit technical, simply move on to the guided tour or one of the three IMAX films on offer. There are two guided tours. If

this is your first visit take the Red Tour which goes to the Apollo Mission and Space Shuttle sites. The Blue Tour goes to Cape Canaveral to see the pioneer space-flight bases. Once you've seen the incredible scale and size of the Shuttle Transporter, the Vehicle Assembly Building and the Saturn V rocket respectively, you'll be in the mood to take off yourself. And if you see the IMAX film, *The Dream is Alive*, then that

(almost) is what you do. IMAX is a special large-scale cinema technique which is projected on to a huge screen – here it is 5 storeys high! Like a simulator it draws you right into the picture and as the Space Shuttle takes off the feeling of power is awesome.

◆
MONTICELLO
Northwest Florida
Those who have a penchant for the Deep South will feel an affinity for this town, named after Thomas Jefferson's Virginia home. It was founded by Georgia and Carolina planters in 1827, and continues to be an agricultural district where watermelons, pecans and satsuma oranges are grown. Visitors come to admire the antebellum (American Civil War period) homes and plantations, the most famous of which is **Bellamy** on State 133. John Bellamy was one of the South Carolina planters who

settled in this part of Florida, but he did more than plant fruit, he laid out Jacksonville and became one of the USA's wealthiest men.

OCALA NATIONAL FOREST
North central Florida
These thousands of acres of wilderness have been nicknamed the 'Big Scrub' due to the numerous sand pine. Located east of Ocala (a region noted for horse farms) and stretching from Oklawaha to St John's River, the Forest is home to hundreds of deer and its streams are a haven for fishermen.

Two popular recreational bases are: Juniper Springs, 26 miles (42km) east of Ocala on State 40, where 8 million gallons (36 million litres) of warm water pour out every day; and Alexander Springs, 16 miles (26km) north of Eustis off State 19, where over 70 million gallons (318 million litres) of water flow daily. Both places are excellent for swimming and canoeing.

OSCEOLA NATIONAL FOREST
Northeast Florida
This expansive forest offers 157,000 acres (63,536 hectares) for camping, fishing or exploring. One favourite base is Ocean Pond, though you could opt for Lake City at the forest edge. Osceola embraces the **Olustee Historic Battlefield Site**, where the only significant Civil War battle on Florida soil was fought. It's worth a visit in February, when costumed participants come from all over the country to re-enact the 1864 conflict.

PALM BEACH
Southeast coast
Both Palm Beach and its neighbour, West Palm Beach are élite resorts on Florida's Gold Coast, the haunts of well-heeled hedonists, where Rolls Royces and credit cards are at their most active.

Not until the Civil War was the first house built in Palm Beach – by a draft dodger – and by 1873 there were still no more than four families. It was probably due to a shipwreck, when coconuts were washed ashore, planted and bore fruit, that this uninspired site was first noticed. In 1880 the settlers christened it Palm Beach. The luxurious look of Palm Beach can be attributed to Addison Mizner, who designed Mediterranean-style homes for the wealthy – and, indeed, created a whole new industry in the area to produce the bright glazed tiles he wanted. The élitist reputation was, however, started by Henry Flagler, the railway mogul, who established Palm Beach as a playground for himself and his rich friends. His pioneer hotel, the Royal Poinciana, quickly became a favourite with Philadelphia society and their stamp of approval led to the construction of other opulent estates and exclusive clubs.

Whitehall, built by Henry Flagler for his third wife (above and detail, right), is now a museum dedicated to the mogul

Flagler's own white marble palatial mansion, **Whitehall**, on Whitehall Way, off Coconut Row, has been restored to its 1902 grandeur and serves as a museum to Flagler's achievements and lifestyle (closed Monday), with his own private railroad car, *The Rambler*, a permanent exhibit in the estate's grounds.
In West Palm Beach, the **Norton Gallery of Art** on South Olive Avenue, has an outstanding collection of paintings and a

particularly fine collection of jade (closed Monday); and in the **South Florida Science Museum** on Dreher Trail, there are hands-on exhibits in the Discovery Hall, underwater life in the aquarium, and stars in the planetarium.

Travel west on Southern Boulevard to reach **Lion Country Safari**, where the big cats and other African wildlife roam uncaged. Elephant and boat rides, camp grounds and a hospitality centre are all part of the complex. The **Dreher Park Zoo** on Summit Boulevard features animals, gardens and nature trails.

The Palm Beaches are noted for their deluxe hotels, such as The Breakers, and quality stores, such as those lining Worth Avenue in the heart of Palm Beach. The glitterati come to watch polo – British royalty play here – and are whisked around in Rolls Royces or Bentleys, to dinner at the Poinciana Club or to the show at the Royal Poinciana Playhouse.

◆
PANAMA CITY
Northwest coast
This is not only an important commercial port city but also a vibrant resort town. Panama City Beach is 30 miles (48km) away across the bay, where there is a whirlwind of constant activity. Children love the **Miracle Strip Amusement Park** (closed in autumn and winter), which adds new rides and attractions each year and includes a giant roller coaster. At **Gulf World** near

the pier, there are continuous daily animal shows (closed in winter). At **Snake-A-Torium** you can learn all about venom extraction and meander around a tropical garden. Other attractions are **Shipwreck Island**, a water theme park on the Miracle Strip (open summer only) and the **Museum of Man in the Sea**, on Back Beach Road, all about the history of underwater exploration.

For a relaxing day's excursion, take a half-hour boat trip from the Captain Anderson Marina to **Shell Island**, a barrier island where you can shell, sunbathe, snorkel or swim; or visit **St Andrews State Recreation Area**, at the eastern tip of Panama City Beach, where there are wide beaches, dunes, wildlife and a restored pioneer turpentine still, as well as nature trails, camping and plenty of sports facilities.

Accommodation ranges from campsites to resort properties. Shopping includes a mall carved out of the 'mountain' attraction, Alvin's Magic Mountain, with restaurants and games rooms as well.

PENSACOLA
Northwest coast
They call it the 'City of Five Flags', and Pensacola has been under the rule of different flags since 1559. This is one of Florida's most historic cities, though today it is a flourishing industrial

centre with a naval station and large, natural landlocked harbour, on the north shore of the Bay. To the east, Bayou Texar and, to the west, Bayou Chico are the wide arms of the bay which reach inland each side of the Pensacola peninsula.

Recorded history begins with Captain Maldonado, commander of the fleet which took De Soto to Florida. The name could stem from the Spanish seaport Peniscola, or from the Indian words *panshi* (hair) and *okla* (people) – once the nickname for the long-haired people who lived here.

History and heritage are today's main attractions no more so than in the **Seville Historic District**. Within this area lies the **Pensacola Historic Village** where visitors can tour through restored homes, art galleries, antique shops and museums (closed Sundays except June to August). The latter includes the **Museum of Commerce**, laid out to resemble a Pensacola Street as it was at the turn of the century, including a trolley car, gas station and several small 'olde worlde' shops. Tucked away in one of Florida's oldest churches, on the corner of Zaragoza Street and Adams Street, is also the **Pensacola Historical Museum**.

The adjacent **Palafox District** includes the region's finest general museum collection, the **TT Wentworth Jr Florida State Museum**, housed in an imposing Italian Revival structure built in 1908 as the Pensacola City Hall. It contains some 30,000 items of local and regional interest plus hands-on exhibits for all the family to enjoy (closed Sunday). Also in this district, on Jefferson Street, is the building that was home to the old city jail. It now houses the **Pensacola Museum of Art** (closed Sunday and Monday).

For more of the same visit the **North Hill Preservation District**, immediately north of the Palafox District. Here you will find a 50-block area where more 18th- and 19th-century homes and historic buildings have been restored. West of town is the Naval Air Station, where the first Navy flyers were trained for World War 1 combat. The **National Museum of Naval Aviation**, one of the three largest aerospace collections in the world, has aircraft from the dawn of flight to a replica of the Skylab Command Module – and it's free! Nearby is the 16th-century Spanish **Fort Barrancas** and the old **Pensacola Lighthouse**. Across the Bay, **Pensacola Beach**, on Santa Rosa Island, offers sugar-white sands and a busy nightlife. **Fort Pickens**, at the island's western tip, saw Civil War action, and served as a prison for Geronimo. Today it is part of the **Gulf Islands National Seashore**, a 150-square mile (388-sq km) stretch of islands and keys, much of which is state protected. Here you can see wildlife – and find a

beach area all to yourself
(recommended for surfers).
For a striking view of Santa
Rosa Island and the Gulf, climb
the observation tower in **Big
Lagoon State Recreation
Area**, a popular woodland
summer spot with an open air
auditorium where concerts are
held.

At unspoiled **Perdido Key**
(situated half-way between
Pensacola and Mobile,
Alabama) a quiet day out can
be spent at Johnson's Beach,

where there's also room to
spread out.

POMPANO BEACH
Southeast coast
This resort is a neighbour to
Fort Lauderdale, but has its
own choice of hotels,
restaurants, nightclubs and
municipal pier (popular for
fishing). Many of its shops are
concentrated around Fashion
Square at 23rd Street, an airy
mall which is well

The USA's oldest house: Gonzalez-Alvarez House, St Augustine

settled until 1565. It became Spain's North American military headquarters and for many years served as Florida's capital. The city was attacked and captured many times, and in 1585 Sir Francis Drake burned it to the ground. Today's visitors are encouraged to take a tour of the city by horse-drawn carriage or sightseeing road train, which can be left and rejoined at will, and perhaps take a cruise of the waterfront.

In St Augustine's restored **Spanish Quarter** on historic George Street, costumed artisans demonstrate the crafts of an earlier era and the narrow streets and restored buildings reflect the Spanish heritage. Just outside the centre, on Magnolia Avenue, is the **Fountain of Youth**, a memorial to Ponce de León, who, according to legend, came to Florida in search of the elusive elixir of youth. The Alcazar hotel on King Street, built by railway tycoon Henry Flagler, is today the **Lightner Museum**, housing superb examples of Tiffany glass as well as mechanical musical instruments and other antiques. The **Oldest House**, on narrow St Francis Street, is a structure combining Spanish, British and American influences. It dates from the early 1600s and is indeed America's oldest house. The **Oldest Schoolhouse** on St George

landscaped and adorned with fine sculptures. Alternatively, try Ocean Side Center, a few yards from the beach. During the winter there is a well-supplied Farmers' Market.

♦♦♦
ST AUGUSTINE ✓

Northeast coast
America's oldest city, St Augustine was discovered by Ponce de León in 1513, but not

Street, built of red cedar and cypress clamped together with wooden pegs, is believed to have been built during the Spanish occupation pre-1763. The **Oldest Store Museum** on Artillery Lane is an authentic turn-of-the-century general store containing 100,000 everyday items of yesteryear.

For those who are interested in American history there is a great deal to see – more than 70 sites in the historic district. Others of note are the beautiful **Ximenez-Fatio House**, built in 1797, and the **Spanish Military Hospital** (both open to the public). The old Ponce de León Hotel, now the **Flagler College**, and the **Flagler Memorial Presbyterian Church** were both built by Henry Flagler in the late 19th century. The Spanish built St Augustine's ornate cathedral in 1797; also of religious interest is the **Shrine of Nuestra Señora de la Leche**, marking the spot where the first mass in America was celebrated. Dominating the entrance to Matanzas Bay is the **Castillo de San Marcos**, North America's oldest masonry fort (begun 1672) with splendid views from its walls. Fourteen miles (23km) south of the city, on Rattlesnake Island,

Castillo de San Marcos, built from shellrock in the 17th century

Henry Flagler's memorial to his daughter: the Presbyterian Church

Fort Matanzas was the site of the bloody 16th-century struggle between French and Spanish colonists, resulting in the slaughter (*matanzas*) of up to 300 French Huguenots.
Museums and collections on the lighter side, include **Potter's Wax Museum** on King Street, and on San Marco Avenue the totally oddball **Ripley's Believe It or Not!**, a treasure trove of trivia, record-breakers and freaks. **St Augustine Alligator Farm**, the state's oldest attraction, with hundreds of alligators and crocodiles and hourly shows, and **Marineland**, with continuous dolphin shows, are both on Route A1A South.

Nature lovers should head out
to **Washington Oaks State
Gardens**, an excellent spot
for bird-watching (at low
tide) and a picnic. A favourite
oceanside park nearer town
is the **Anastasia Recreation
Area** at St Augustine Beach,
featuring acres of beaches,
dunes and a lagoon.

◆

SINGER ISLAND
A delightful spot, only a 15-
minute drive north of Palm
Beach, but not such an
expensive place to stay. The
proximity of the Gulf Stream
keeps temperatures constant –
cooler in summer and
warmer in winter than many
other parts of the state. The
beautiful, wide public beach is
a big draw and all types of
watersports are available.

◆◆◆
SARASOTA ✓

West coast
A cultural city 53 miles (85km)
south of Tampa, Sarasota may
be reached via the scenic
route along Gulf Drive from
the barrier islands, or the
faster I–75.
There is a good choice of
white-sand beaches, not only
on the offshore islands but also
at the bays and small inlets
indenting the coast. The city
itself has its own brand of
charm, enough to have
tempted circus entrepreneur
John Ringling to build his dream
home here: **Ca'D'Zan** and its
38-acre (15-hectare) estate is
today part of the **Ringling
Museums**.

The Ringlings amassed
magnificent tapestries and art
works which can now be
seen at the estate's
Museum of Art, though
undoubtedly youngsters will
prefer the Circus Galleries.

Ca'D'Zan, the exotic Ringling house

Also on the site is the Asolo Theater, an 18th-century Italian theatre dismantled by Ringling, brought to the US and reconstructed here in 1950. Opposite the Ringling Museums, **Bellm's Cars and**

Music of Yesterday contains a fascinating collection of vintage cars, nickelodeons, phonographs and antique arcade games.

In the **Sarasota Jungle
Gardens**, on Bayshore Road,
visitors can look out for
alligators, mina birds, macaws,
and flamingos amidst
thousands of palms and
flowering shrubs.
Fishing is highly regarded in
the Sarasota vicinity, whether
from a beach, a boat or in the
Myakka River State Park, a
wildlife reserve about 14
miles (23km) east of town on
Florida 72. A paved road
winds through most of the
park, a train operates to the
bird observation tower, and
guided boat tours may be
taken.

◆◆
TALLAHASSEE
Northeast Florida
Tallahassee was chosen as
capital of Florida in 1824 and
despite the fact that half the
state population now live
south of Orlando, it is still the

The capitol complex, Tallahassee, Florida's capital since 1824

Civil War – and there are many fine mansions. The oldest house in town is **The Columns** at the junction of North Adam Street and West Park Street, constructed in 1830. It is now the headquarters of the Chamber of Commerce and functions as a visitor information centre. Sightseers should not miss a tour of the old **State Capitol** (1902), situated beside the new Capitol (1977), on a terraced knoll overlooking the business district (New Capitol open Monday to Friday only). On Mondays, Wednesdays and Fridays, tours may be made of the **Florida Governor's Mansion**, which is patterned after Andrew Jackson's Tennessee home, 'The Hermitage'. Historic artefacts and treasures may be viewed at the **Museum of Florida History** on S Bronough Street. The **Tallahassee Museum of History and Natural Science**, near the airport, features nature trails and an 1880 pioneer farm, and is also a refuge for the endangered Florida panther.

Winter is probably the best time to see **Alfred B Maclay State Ornamental Garden**, north of town on US319, when azaleas and other native flowers are in full bloom. South of town, off SR61, at **Wakulla Springs State Park**, thousands of gallons of water flow each minute from underground caverns to form

legislative and administrative centre.

When the Spaniards arrived in 1539, Tallahassee was a flourishing Apalachee Indian settlement. The site of the former Indian village and Spanish Mission is now the **San Luis Archaeological Site**, on W Mission Road.

The atmosphere of the town is very southern – it was never captured during the

Historic US space craft at the Kennedy Space Center

the Wakulla River, upon which glass bottom boat rides are offered. **Lake Jackson Indian Mounds**, on the shore of Lake Jackson, cover a small area but are of interest to historians, as many Indian temple mounds have been uncovered here.

Tallahassee is also the location of one of Florida's few vineyards, Lafayette Vineyards & Winery, on Mahan Drive, where tours and tastings are available.

◆◆
WEEKI WACHEE SPRING
This famous family attraction is on US19 and Florida 50, 13 miles (21km) west of Brooksville. Centred around a 130-foot (40-m) deep clear natural spring, it's the place to watch fascinating underwater shows given by 'mermaids'; performing swimmers who breathe via submerged air lines. Glass-bottom boat tours make the most of the crystal-clear waters and beautiful scenery and there's a waterpark adjacent where you can cool off (late March to September).

PEACE AND QUIET

Countryside and Wildlife in Florida
by Paul Sterry

Although Florida's summers can be extremely hot and humid, the winters are mild, and this attracts large numbers of visitors from September to May. Florida's wildlife also benefits from the sub-tropical climate and many of its plants and animals depend upon the mild weather.

Mangrove swamps line the undeveloped stretches of the coast and many of the plants found inland would look equally at home in a South American forest. The birds, too, tend to be more exotic than their counterparts in the rest of the USA. Resident species are supplemented during the winter months by migratory birds from Canada and the northern USA escaping the ravages of the freezing north. The warm climate also favours cold-blooded animals such as reptiles, amphibians and insects. Most conspicuous of these is the American alligator. Florida juts into the sea, with the Atlantic on the east and the Gulf of Mexico on the west. Because of the extensive coastline and favourable climate, much of the coast has been developed into resorts and facilities for tourism. However, despite this, much of interest can still be seen, even among the marinas and other developments.

Tropical plants such as palms flourish in Florida's parks

PEACE AND QUIET

The Everglades

Florida's southern tip is dominated by the Everglades, a vast wilderness of shallow marsh and grassland covering more than 1½ million acres (0.6 million hectares). Because of the vast distances involved, a car is essential to do justice to the Everglades.

Although interesting throughout the year, the Everglades are most rewarding during the winter months. This is considered to be the dry season and, as the waters recede, so the animals are obliged to congregate around those pools and lakes which remain. Having entered from the park's southern gate, one of the first stops is the Royal Palm Visitor Center. From here you can follow the well-signposted Anhinga Trail, which is only a ½ mile (0.8km) long, but is generally full of interest. Alongside the boardwalk anhingas nest, feed and sunbathe. These primitive-looking birds do not have waterproof feathers, despite their aquatic life-style. Consequently, they have to dry their wings in the sunshine at regular intervals. Alligators on this trail mostly cruise around the water channels but they do occasionally venture up on to the walkways so keep your eyes open!

The reason for the abundance of fish-eating birds and alligators in the Everglades soon becomes apparent when you watch the water, it simply teems with life. The tiny torpedo-shaped garfish is the most abundant species, but bass and sunfish are also much in evidence. Equally abundant are terrapins and frogs which also feature highly in the diets of the birds and alligators. From the main entrance to the Everglades, a road runs south for 36 miles (58km), with plenty to see en route.

Birds of prey are a conspicuous feature of the skies, riding the thermals as soon as the sun warms the ground. Black vultures and turkey vultures are exceedingly common and sometimes feed off carrion beside the road. More elegant

is the red-shouldered hawk, which often perches beside the road on low bushes or telegraph poles. It is sometimes joined by that most graceful of raptors, the swallowed-tailed kite, which is a summer resident in the Everglades and extremely restricted in its distribution. A variety of mammals can also be seen from the road. Dawn and dusk are the best times to look for white-tailed deer which often graze the grass on the roadside. The charming little marsh rabbit also feeds along the roadside. A night-time drive through the park may reveal the more secretive, nocturnal residents of the Everglades. Several ponds and lakes lie beside FL27. Paurotis Pond and Nine Mile Pond, on the right and left of the road respectively, are good for wildfowl. Mrazek Pond, 4 miles (6.5km) before Flamingo on the right, and Eco Pond, 1 mile (1.6km) beyond, are small and allow close views of the birds. Water conditions vary from day to

American alligators are common throughout the Everglades

day in each stretch of water, so it is difficult to predict exactly what will be where. However, you are sure to see snowy egrets with their characteristic yellow 'socks', tiny green herons and the inevitable alligator. If you are lucky you may see the aptly-named roseate spoonbill with its strangely flattened bill. Unfortunately, flamingos no longer grace the lakes and shores of Florida, so any large pink bird you see is likely to be a spoonbill.

An alternative point of access to the Everglades is at Shark Valley, on the park's northern boundary. From here you can follow a circular route of 15 miles (24km) along a made-up track through the heart of the Everglades. You can walk the trail, but an interesting mode of transport is to hire a bike and pedal around. The alligators are the most astonishing

feature of this trail. Every pool has its own resident and some of them exceed 10 feet (3m) in length. They are most frequently seen sunbathing beside the pool, with their mouths open to help dissipate excess heat. You can sometimes pass within a few feet of these great animals, but it is advisable to steer well clear of them.

There are a number of larger bodies of water in this part of the Everglades, known as 'sloughs'. Needless to say, they are a haven for fish and alligators, but they also attract water snakes, which feast on the tadpoles and small fish they contain. Alligators are instrumental in keeping these sloughs open and free from vegetation. Their vigorous wallowing helps prevent plants

Tricoloured herons stalk their prey around watery margins

from colonising the water margins. However, the spikes of the colourful water plant, pontederia, manage to add a splash of purple to the margins of most pools and sloughs.

On hot days, snakes are often seen crossing the made-up track. Largest and most venomous of these is the Florida cottonmouth, a relative of the rattlesnake but without the rattle. If cornered, these snakes coil up and gape, revealing the soft, white mouths which gave them their name. However, cornering a cottonmouth is not to be recommended!

The road which runs along the northern boundary of the park is a good place to watch herons and egrets as they feed in the drainage ditches, but is especially renowned for being the best place to view the scarce Everglade or snail kite. This bird flies gracefully over the reeds, occasionally revealing its white rump, while in search of its staple diet, the apple snail. The kite's elongated, curved bill is the perfect tool for winkling the snail out of its shell. The road is also a good spot to watch flights of birds at dawn and dusk as they fly to and from their feeding and roosting grounds.

Ponds and Lakes

There are ponds and lakes throughout Florida and they all act as magnets for wildlife. Although they may vary in size, from the massive Lake Okeechobee in central Florida, to the tiny pools of the Everglades, they are all sure to be worth a visit.

Most ponds and lakes have a margin of reeds and other water plants. These serve as convenient perches for the wealth of water birds which congregate to feed on the fish and amphibians. Largest and most conspicuous of these are the herons and egrets. In addition to the ubiquitous snowy egrets and green herons, patient watching should reveal tricoloured and little blue herons and perhaps even a bittern.

Birdwatching around ponds and lakes in Florida has an advantage over many other areas, in that binoculars are not often needed. Indeed, they can be a positive disadvantage because the birds frequently come too close!

Although many species have lost their fear of man, they still recognise danger in other forms. Despite their long legs, adapted for wading in deep water, almost all the herons and egrets perch above the water, plunging in only when a meal is on offer. The reason for this apparently peculiar behaviour, which is not observed in the same species elsewhere in the USA, becomes obvious when you begin to appreciate the number of alligators and snapping turtles that most of the pools hold: to wade in the water is to invite trouble.

American coots are common around the margins of most ponds and lakes. Although superficially similar to their European relatives, a close look reveals a distinctive black

PEACE AND QUIET

mark on the bill and white feathers under the tail. If you are very fortunate, they may be joined by their relative, the American purple gallinule. Generally secretive creatures, gallinules do sometimes venture into the open at dawn to bask in the first rays of sun. Ponds and lakes can be found throughout Florida and most have typical wetland wildlife. Try visiting Loxahatchee National Wildlife Refuge inland from Delray Beach. A visitor centre and nature trails can be found off US441 between SR804 and SR806. In Fort Lauderdale, visit Royal Palm Park on NW 38th Street at NW 17th Avenue, and Rookery Lake Sanctuary on FL27. Lake Okechobee, on FL27 between Palmdale and Clewiston, is also good.

Tropical Forests

Throughout the Everglades and around much of the coast of Florida are found small pockets of tropical forest. Interestingly, they contain species of plants and animals which have closer links with South America than with the temperate forests in neighbouring states of the USA. Many of these forests, referred to as 'hammocks' in the Everglades, are only a few acres in area and are isolated in a sea of grassland, and yet the ages of the trees bear witness to their long-term survival.

Hammocks tend to grow on limestone outcrops and are usually a few feet above the surrounding land. This slight elevation may not seem particularly significant but it provides enough long-term stability to allow trees to grow to a large size. During the wet season, most of the surrounding land is inundated with water, which discourages all but the hardiest of grasses. By contrast, during the dry season, the hammocks retain a lot of moisture in the soil surrounding the roots. As a consequence they are less prone to damage from the dry season fires which can sweep through the surrounding grassland.

Many of the tropical hammocks in the Everglades have boardwalks giving visitors access to the forest while at the same time preventing damage to the vegetation. Entering a hammock is like walking into a different world. Gone is the intense heat of the sun, replaced with dappled sunlight and cool, humid air. Strangler figs grapple their way up their hosts' trunks towards the tree canopy, eventually to constrict their benefactors to death. At ground level, prickly pear cacti grow in clearings, while above them the branches and trunks of the trees are festooned with epiphytic plants – plants without roots in soil which grow instead on other plants. In most cases the epiphytes cause no direct harm to the plant they live on, apart from adding to its weight. Most striking of these plants are the bromeliads, or 'air-plants', with spiky rosettes of leaves and colourful flowers.

Good examples of 'hammocks' of tropical forest can be found along the Gumbo Limbo trail at Royal Palm Hammock, just beyond the visitor centre for the Everglades National Park. Also visit Mahogany Hammock, one mile (1.6km) west of FL27, approximately 20 miles (32km) beyond the visitor centre.

The Keys

The Keys conjure up romantic images of the Caribbean, with exotic beaches and aquamarine seas. The reality is different. Development has encroached on all but a few pockets of natural vegetation. However, it is not all bad news; almost every golf course has a thriving population of burrowing owls and white ibises adorning the greens. The Keys are a chain of islands which stretch south from the tip of Florida for nearly 90 miles (145km). Nowadays, a road (US1) – one of the world's longest over-water roads – links them all making it possible to drive from Miami to Key West in a day. Along most of the route there are power lines and telegraph poles, which serve as perches for the exotic scissor-tailed flycatcher, a regular winter visitor. Waders and terns are common and a careful eye on the skies should eventually reveal a truly exotic speciality of the Keys, the magnificent frigatebird. With a wingspan of over 8 feet (2.5m), these birds soar effortlessly on the sea breeze, harassing other seabirds into regurgitating their last meal, which the frigatebirds then catch and eat! However, the most spectacular bird of the

Keys must surely be the great white heron, an immense bird which stands nearly 5 feet (1.5m) tall and is only to be found here. There are still a few remnants of natural vegetation to be seen, such as mangrove swamps and slash pine forests. The best examples are to be found on Big Pine Key, where there are several wildlife refuges and the undergrowth includes an endemic species of prickly pear, Spanish moss and exotic-looking yuccas.

Key Deer

Visitors keen to see the diminutive and endearing Key deer should visit Big Pine Key. This dog-sized animal has its only stronghold on this Key. Small groups often venture out of the undergrowth at dusk to browse beside the road and provide a charming sight. Visitors should be particularly careful when driving on Big Pine Key because unfortunately dozens of these fragile creatures are accidentally killed each year by cars.

A stately great white heron

Cypress Swamps

Many of Florida's wet woodland areas have been drained, but a few still survive under the protection of a variety of conservation organisations. The wettest woodlands are known as cypress swamps. Perhaps the best example is the National Audubon Society's Corkscrew Swamp, near the small town of Immokalee.

The drier parts of the wood are composed of slash pine, but as the water level rises this gives way to cypresses. The trees are festooned with exotic epiphytic orchids, ferns and lichens, with great creepers reaching for the skies. Fortunate visitors may see the elusive river otter but the Florida fox squirrel is more conspicuous, distinguished by its black face. Birds, too, are abundant in Corkscrew Swamp. The large and noisy pileated woodpecker drills dead timber in search of grubs. Herons and egrets stalk fish in the open channels of water. Little blue herons are often seen trotting across the carpets of water lettuce and there are a few pairs of wood storks nesting in trees. At dawn and dusk the feeding birds are sometimes joined by a limpkin, a secretive ibis-like bird whose extraordinary nocturnal calls are very definitive.

As the cypress trees age they die and fall, leaving stumps which gradually become eroded into pinnacles of wood. These provide ideal perches for the barred owl, one of the most spectacular birds to be seen in this habitat.

Pine Forests

Pine forests are widespread throughout the state of Florida. Three of the largest forests are the Apalachicola National Forest (557,000 acres/225,412 hectares) in the northwest, the Ocala National Forest (366,000 acres/418,116 hectares) north of Orlando and the Osceola National Forest (157,000 acres/63,536 hectares) near Lake City. Seven species of native pine occur in Florida, but the slash pine predominates.

A carpet of fallen pine needles and cabbage palms prevents an extensive ground flora developing, but spikes of lady's tresses orchids can be seen. Common anole lizards and skinks scuttle amongst the ground vegetation and several species of snake are found in most woodlands.

Woodlands contain many species of mammal. The well-named armadillo roots in the soil for food and can occasionally be located by this sound, but the bobcat is much quieter and a good deal of luck will be needed to see one. Listen for rustling in the ground vegetation and you may see a party of boldly marked bobwhite quails.

Shell Collecting

A description of Florida would not be complete without mentioning the shells for which the state is famous. Almost every beach has a good selection but those Sanibel, Captiva, Cape Sable and Marathon Key are renowned, and the remarkable sub-tropical shells such as conches, murex and couries immediately catch the eye. Regrettably, many keen shell collectors are only interested in the shells of living animals. Many species are under threat, so that in certain areas collectors are restricted to two live animals of each species. In any case, if they are not to be found on the beaches, there are innumerable stores selling shells.

Screw pine on the Florida Keys (below) and a barred owl (above)

FOOD AND DRINK

FOOD AND DRINK

Think of orange juice and you think of Florida, for the state claims to produce 25 per cent of the world's orange crop and 95 per cent of all orange juice concentrate. Fresh fruit is readily available. Orlando was an early citrus centre – and indeed, there are still groves upon groves in the area. Exotic fruits have joined the more common variety, and interesting jams, marmalades and chutneys are for sale in the gourmet food shops.

In recent years, the state has been experimenting with fruit wines, but there are perhaps not enough accolades to warrant recommendation. Do

About a third of Florida's agricultural yield comes from oranges, grapefruit and tangerines

look out, though, for the local (albeit rare) white tupelo honey.

As in so many US destinations, the cattle industry was big business in Florida, an important preface to agriculture, and beef is still a menu staple. But it is with seafood that this state comes into its own.

Florida's waters have always provided a steady food supply. Even the earliest settlers did not lack for shellfish, but it was the development of quick-freezing processes which made seafood and freshwater fish production a commercial industry.

You can hardly go wrong dining out at one of Florida's countless fish restaurants, where there is a choice of clams, shrimp, oysters, mullet and snapper or local lobster (crawfish). Scamp, by the way, is not a misspelling of scampi, but a fish in its own right – white and flaky and related to the grouper family. It is scarce, but try it if you have the chance. Stone crabs are another delicacy, in season in winter and a speciality at several Miami establishments.

Ethnic Food

Florida's food is as diverse as the people who live there. There are only remnants of native Indian cuisine, such as cassava pie and corn fritters, but the Cubans, who have considerably swelled the population, have brought their taste for spicy fare with them. That means black beans with everything and sweet black coffee afterwards. The influence is at its strongest in Calle Ocho in Miami and in Ybor City, the Latin section of Tampa.

There is also a sizeable Greek community centred around Tarpon Springs, where so many tavernas are serving up moussaka and keftedes it seems like a mini Athens! Down in the Keys, look on menus for conch fritters and Key Lime pie. The conch (pronounced 'conk') is a bland edible mollusc. It is also the colloquial name given to island-born Key Westers, who are descendants of a Cuban, Yankee seafarer and British loyalist mix. Key Lime pie – now popular throughout the States – should, if it's authentic, be coloured cream, not bright green.

In St Augustine, you may notice a Spanish influence on some of the restaurant menus – highly seasoned stews made with chicken, pork and seafood mixed with rice, beans and peppers. You can also find cheese turnovers and *picadillo*, seasoned ground beef mixed with olives, raisins and onions.

Happy Eating

Remember that whatever food you order, portions are bound to be hefty – far more so than in Europe. Americans tend to feel they are not getting their money's worth unless a plate is piled high. In some cases, this means they would rather settle for one dish rather than follow the European penchant for a three of four course meal. This can work in tourists' favour – it is acceptable, for example, to ask for one dessert and four forks. All-you-can-eat salad bars offer a choice of salad which is large and varied, and everything is always extremely fresh and crisp.

Fast food restaurants often feature all-you-can-eat-platters (sometimes seafood), which can be a saving when you are travelling with hungry, growing youngsters, while adults may take advantage of free canapés provided by cocktail lounges at 'Happy Hour' (usually 5.30 to 7.30pm).

SHOPPING

Because Americans themselves have a passion for shopping, visitors won't lack for places to buy or browse. Wherever there's a spare niche, there's a boutique or souvenir stand; wherever there's space, a new mall or shopping centre goes up. Renewed preservation efforts continue into the 1990s and more and more historic districts are being restored. They are not registered for architectural interest but include conversions to gift shops and art galleries. Many shopping areas are designed with a theme (a fishing village, perhaps), or reflect an ethnic character (Greek in Tarpon Springs, Cuban in Ybor City) or a particular era (Victorian period).

Some are particularly famous, like Coral Gables' Miracle Mile where all the leading American brand names in clothing are sold. Your budget may not stretch to the prices in the windows along Las Olas Boulevard in Fort Lauderdale or Worth Avenue in Palm Beach, but who can resist a saunter down either? A long established, but still chic Miami area, is Bal Harbour, with notable department stores such as Saks and

A replica of HMS Bounty, *scene of a 1789 mutiny, lies in Biscayne Bay*

Neiman-Marcus. Coconut Grove, south of Miami, is Florida's very own Greenwich Village, with hundreds of upmarket shops and restaurants.

One of the best ethnic areas is Calle Ocho in downtown Miami (South West 8th Street) which has been developed as Miami's Latin Quarter. Here you'll find bakeries selling sweet Cuban pastries and small cigar factories where the product is still hand rolled. Ybor City is Tampa's picturesque Latin Quarter, and here, too, new life has been injected. Ybor Square's shops, now brim with antiques, arts and plants, and many new additions are expected. Its 'Nostalgia Market' offers bygones from stalls.

The pride of Miami is Bayside Marketplace, a $93 million waterfront speciality shopping centre where you'll find up-market boutiques as well as international food stands and restaurants. Downtown Orlando's popular Church Street Station also offers some excellent specialty shopping in its Church Street Exchange, a festive three-level shopping area in Victorian style. America is famous for its discount centres and factory outlets, where you can pick up brand named goods for a lesser price than in the *de luxe* stores. It is best to look at local tourist publications and newspapers when you arrive in Florida, whatever your base, but to give you some idea, the Quality Outlet Center on International Drive in Orlando features brand name factory outlets which include Corning (a respectable name for kitchenware), top labelled men's clothing, Great Western Boots and top women's fashions.

Since Orlando and its vicinity is likely to take top priority on your holiday itinerary, it is worth visiting the Florida Mall at the intersection of 441 and 482 for its 200 stores; Maingate Mall in Kissimmee (close to the Magic Kingdom entrance) with more than 80 stores; and Osceola Square Mall, 84 stores on West Highway 192 in Kissimmee. Also in Kissimmee, Old Town, designed in turn-of-the-century style, is a well-established tourist attraction featuring over 100 shops. Theme parks also provide an infinite variety of shops. At Walt Disney World, for example, all the resort hotels have their own shops, as does Magic Kingdom's Main Street USA and EPCOT's World Showcase pavilions (don't spend too much valuable time shopping within the theme parks, however, as there is so much to see). Then there's Walt Disney World Shopping Village, where boutiques sell a variety of merchandise from Christmas decorations to children's wear and nautical gifts. Disney soft toys are, of course, in abundant supply. There are also shopping bazaars in the Morocco and Stanleyville sections of the Busch Gardens theme park near Tampa. All sorts of cooking ingredients can be bought here which are difficult to find anywhere else. Resort wear is always a good buy – every imaginable oddity seems to be available, and clothing of all kinds is stocked in a wide range of sizes.

You could buy your sponges in Greece, but Tarpon Springs' infinite variety, from back scratchers to car washers, are equally good value. You could buy your cigars in Cuba, but Miami's Latin Quarter and Tampa's Ybor City have their own ample supplies. You could buy your shells in the Caribbean but they're much cheaper in the Gulf islands off Florida. And the varieties of exotic jams and chutneys in American country stores are hard to resist.

The US is the land of the credit card which makes shopping in Florida a convenient as well as an exciting experience.

ACCOMMODATION

Florida accommodation runs the gamut from budget motels to plush resorts as well as a growing number of all-suite properties. Motels offer particularly good value for families (the better ones have restaurant and recreational facilities) since one price pays for a room that can often sleep four people.

They are located along the state highways and beaches and close to popular visitor areas like Walt Disney World and all resorts. A number of them are members of a chain such as Hilton, Howard Johnson or Day's Inn, all of a reasonable standard. Self-catering holiday apartments and villas are an alternative way of keeping costs down and the choice is enormous. Here again, general standards are high – flats are often situated in complexes with their own swimming pools and other sports facilities.

Bed and breakfast in private homes is available, but most of these associations are not represented outside of the US and it is necessary to contact them direct. Bear in mind that b&b in America is often more expensive than a motel.

There are plenty of glamorous resort hotels in Florida, especially on the east coast, if cost is not of prime importance. Don't forget that the word 'resort' as applied to an American hotel implies a luxury complex with every conceivable facility on site – it does not mean a holiday destination.

NIGHTLIFE

There is no shortage of cultural and light entertainment in the cities, where there are numerous performing arts centres, theatres and nightclubs. Top name entertainers frequently appear in Miami at the large hotels, and clubs here often feature lavish revues. Nightlife is also lively in the Orlando area, including Walt Disney World itself. Details of current shows are available in local papers and visitor publications.

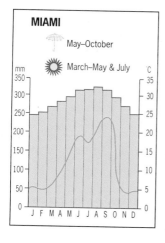

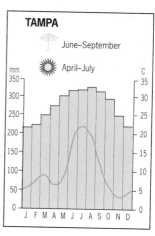

WEATHER AND WHEN TO GO

Although summer temperatures are pretty uniform in all parts of Florida – probably in the 80s F (30s C), winter climates can vary. Average January temperatures, for example, range from around 50° F (10° C) in the northwest to 64° F (18° C) along the lower coast and 70° F (21° C) in the Keys. In the brief cool winter, coastal regions will be warmer than inland, due to the influence of the Gulf and Atlantic. Rainfall is heaviest from July to October.

The top luxury resort hotels will expect some formality of dress in the evening although the jacket and tie rule is nowadays very much the exception. Normally, summer resort wear that is cool, casual and comfortable, is more than adequate. Add a wrap, jacket or sweater for the odd cool winter spell or as a precaution against icy air-conditioning.

CHILDREN

If there is one American state which specifically appeals to children, that state is Florida. There are so many theme parks and family-orientated attractions that the choice is almost overpowering. The Orlando area alone is unrivalled. Walt Disney World quite apart, there is a host of water theme parks, animal and bird shows, wax museums, alligator centres, amusement arcades, thrill rides, zoos and marine parks. But be selective; entrance fees can mount up. In the case of the best known attractions (Walt Disney World, Sea World, Universal Studios, Cypress Gardens, Busch Gardens, etc) charges are high, but they do cover all the rides and attractions for a whole day. In some cases passes are included in holiday packages.

Florida's beach choice is huge, too. The offshore islands to the west are unspoiled and quiet and will not be suited to active youngsters who like fairgrounds and video arcades, nor is there much to do in most of the Keys apart from watersports. Both the Pinellas and the Gold Coast resorts, however, have enough to please all ages.

America's museums are based on the principle that education should be fun, and in Florida they often encourage visitor participation with hands-on exhibits. Science museums always feature such galleries, and often boast a planetarium as well. History is brought alive by the use of craft and other demonstrations, and costumed guides. Other cultural heritage is handled similarly – at Florida's Indian villages for example. Americans love to spoil children – and there is plenty to keep them occupied in the Sunshine State.

FESTIVALS AND EVENTS

Innumerable festivals and events take place all over Florida. Local newspapers and visitor publications will tell you what's on. Among the highlights are:

A touch of tropical colour from a macaw in Cypress Gardens

JANUARY
Daytona Beach – 24 Hour Race
Homestead – Annual Rodeo
Miami Beach – Art Deco Weekend
Coral Gables – Miracle Mile Art Show
West Palm Beach – Polo & Country Club Season, Silver Sailfish Derby
Orlando – Highland Games
Sarasota – Annual Shell Show
Key West – Art Expo Craft Show

FEBRUARY
Palatka – Azalea Festival
Olustee – Battle of Olustee
St Augustine – Menendez Day
Daytona Beach – Daytona 500
Coconut Grove – Arts Festival
Miami Beach – Arts Festival
Miami – Grand Prix and International Festival, Boat Show

Key West – Old Island Days
Orlando – Central Florida Fair
Winter Haven – Florida Citrus Festival
Sarasota – Asolo State Theater Season
Fort Myers Beach – Estero Island Shrimp Festival
Plant City – Florida Strawberry Festival
Tampa – Gasparilla Pirate Invasion, Ybor City Fiesta Day

MARCH

Miami – Renaissance Fair
Daytona Beach – Cycle Week
Miami – Calle Ocho Open House, Carnaval Miami
Fort Lauderdale – Las Olas Art Festival
Lignumvitae Key – Lignumvitae Blossom Festival
West Palm Beach – Arts Festival
Orlando – Central Florida Fair
Arcadia – All-Florida Championship Rodeo
Dunedin – Highland Games
Tampa – Latin American Fiesta
Sanibel Island – Shell Fair
Kissimmee – Blue Grass Festival
Sarasota – Medieval Fair
Fort Myers – Shrimp Festival

APRIL

St Augustine – Arts & Crafts Festival, Blessing of the Fleet
Palatka – District Rodeo
Jacksonville and Dunedin – Highland Games
Daytona Beach – Music Festival

MAY

Miami – Seafood Festival, Miami River Regatta
Sarasota – International Sandcastle Contest

Pensacola – Festival of Five Flags

JUNE

Daytona Beach – Summer Speed Week
Coconut Grove – Goombay Festival
Miami Beach – Indoor Flea Market

JULY

Daytona Beach – Firecracker 400, Paul Devere 250
Miami – Outdoor Music Festival
Key West – Hemingway Days
Kissimmee – Silver Spurs Rodeo
Arcadia – All-Florida Rodeo

AUGUST

Boca Raton – Boca Festival
Fort Walton Beach – Billfish Tournament

SEPTEMBER

Cocoa Beach – Florida Pro International Surfing Contest
Key West – Oyster Season

OCTOBER

Miami – Hispanic Heritage Festival
Miami and Orlando – Oktoberfests
Key West – Fantasy Fest

NOVEMBER

St Augustine – Fall Arts & Crafts Festival
Miami – Greek Festival, Arts Festival
Orlando – Light up Orlando
Apalachicola – Florida Seafood Festival

DECEMBER

Miami – King Orange Jamboree Parade

HOW TO BE A LOCAL

If you happen to have blue rinsed hair and don't mind whether or not you look good in a colourful shirt or shift, you will certainly fit into the Miami or St Petersburg picture very well.

Many so-called Floridians, known around here as 'Snowbirds', have actually retired here from colder climes.

But the really local populace is both young and fun loving, favouring the outdoor life and tootling about on boats. No more so than in the Keys where the pace is particularly laid back. The average Floridian is usually sporty, but just as keen to dabble in a spot of fishing as to take it seriously.

Whatever your age, if you're young at heart, you'll be delighted by Florida and Florida will be delighted by you. It may have been outsiders who saw the potential and developed the plethora of theme parks, but the residents have a child-like joy about them too. Though many of the attractions are man-made, natural ones haven't been destroyed and wildlife is left in peace in the giant tracts of swamp and forest that covers chunks of the state.

If you love the feeling of sand between your toes, the taste of succulent seafood and can let your hair down on a whim, you're well on the way to becoming Floridianised – it's a state of mind.

TIGHT BUDGET TIPS

- The easiest way to save money is to pick up discount coupons, available at your hotel, from tourist information centres, local newspapers, etc. These give money off eating out ,accommodation, shopping, and all attractions except Walt Disney World (if anyone does claim to be able to do this then beware, there is a catch, usually involving time-share selling). In Orlando make your first stop the Visitor Center at the Mercado Mediterranean Village to pick up a free Orlando Magicard – a coupon booklet in credit card format.

- If there are four in a family, stay at a place which can provide two double beds in one room, so that children can stay with parents for the same price (age limits can vary from 12 to18).

- Eat fast food – it may not be elegant, but it is economical. Look out for fixed-price all-you-can-eat signs. Diners offer excellent value for breakfast and early-evening meals. American portions are huge so don't have a starter.

- If you want to hire a car, do some homework – many tour operators offer very good fly/drive deals. Otherwise you could find that small local firms offer cheaper rental rates than some of the big international companies. Beware, however, of hidden insurance extras.

- Entrance fees to theme parksmount up. Make a top-priority list and stick to it.

DIRECTORY

Arriving

Florida boasts three main international airports. Miami is the major air terminal for Florida, with direct flights from many international airports. Tampa, serving Florida's Gulf Coast area, has flight connections with Europe and South America. Orlando, serving Florida's interior resort areas, has been the fastest growing airport and is considered the most modern and best planned. It is served by over 24 carriers with direct services from over 100 cities worldwide. Most US airlines, schedule regular flights into Florida. Air connection between Florida cities are frequent. Those who plan to travel around the state by air should purchase tickets on a Visit USA fare structure. Flights between points such as Miami and the Keys are reasonably priced, but planes are small and bookings can be heavy.
Travel Documents Visas are not required by EU citizens wishing to stay less than 90 days, provided that a return or onward ticket is held. A current full passport is, of course, necessary (a visitor's passport is insufficient). Visa waiver forms are distributed inflight, along with customs declarations – these must be completed and handed in at immigration control on arrival. It is best to check the requirements for specific holiday plans with your travel agent or the nearest US embassy, consulate or tourism office before departure. The Americans are strict in these matters and passengers whose travel documents are not in order will not be accepted in the US under any circumstances.

Camping

Florida has more campgrounds and campsites than any other state. They are to be found in almost every national or state park, forest and recreational area, including Walt Disney World. Most are open all year and have electrical hook-ups, supplies store and leisure facilities. The *Florida Camping Directory*, published annually, gives full details of some of the best campgrounds/sites; it is available free, from Florida Campground Association, Department D–8, 1638 N Plaza Drive, Tallahassee, FL 32308-5323 (tel: (904) 656 8878).

Car Breakdown

See **International Motoring Benefits**

Car Hire

See **Domestic Travel** (sub-heading, **Driving** – page 121)

Chauffeur Driven Cars

Easy to arrange but not cheap. Some hotels and motels in the tourist areas provide a complimentary limousine service to and from airports. A 'public' limousine service performs a shuttle service between airport and hotel for less than the cost of a taxi, but should not be confused with the more luxurious,

Florida has plenty of car hire choice – and the lowest US prices

sedan-type, private limousine. Bookings for chauffeur drive for US destinations may be made in advance through one of the international car rental companies.

Crime

Like most cosmopolitan areas, crime is rife in Florida, and holiday-makers can be easy targets. Make your trip incident-free by following these simple safety rules: stay alert; never leave bags unattended or visible in your car; use travellers' cheques or credit cards instead of cash; try a money belt or bum bag instead of a handbag; only use cashpoints in well-lit public areas; never stop or wind down your window if you are flagged down, unless by the police. If your car is hit from behind do not stop. Drive to the nearest police station or flag down a police officer.

Customs Regulations

You will be handed a customs declaration form during your flight, which should be completed and given to Customs on arrival. The form should list everything brought into the US, whether gifts for others or not. There is no limit to the amount of cash or travellers' cheques brought in or out of the country. Customs regulations are under review, but at present they allow: 200 cigarettes, 100 cigars and 1 litre of spirits. Note that these are for those aged 21 or over. Not allowed: drugs (other than prescribed), fresh meat, fruit and plants.

Disabled Travellers

Resort hotels, larger restaurants, theme parks and other popular areas generally cater well for disabled people – you will invariably find ramps, wide doors, lifts and other wheelchair provisions. Some hotels also have specially designed phones suitable for hearing-impaired people.

A comprehensive brochure, *The Physically Challenged Guide to Florida*, is available from the Florida Department of Commerce, Division of Tourism, Visitor Enquiry, 107 West Gaines Street, Collins Building, Tallahassee, FL 32399–2000 (tel: (904) 488

7598. It lists the names and addresses of organisations that can help the disabled traveller.

Domestic Travel

Air (see **Arriving**)

Driving You need a valid driving licence to rent a car in Florida, though an International Driving Permit is required for visitors from certain countries. You must be 21 or over, but you will have difficulty finding a company if you are under 25 or you may have to pay a significantly higher insurance premium. Florida, like the rest of the US, has an extensive and up-to-date system of freeways (motorways) and highways (other roads). Superhighways are toll roads charging a few cents a mile, and petrol remains more reasonable than in many other destinations. The speed limit is either 55 miles (88km) per hour or 65 miles (104km) per hour. In cities and congested areas though it is generally between 20–40 miles (32–64km) per hour and 15 miles (24km) per hour in school zones. Road signs indicate specific limits and these are strictly enforced. Driving is on the right. Two peculiarities to American driving are that it is permitted for a motorist to filter right at a red traffic light after stopping (a flashing red light means stop, then proceed with caution in any direction), and that traffic in both directions must stop while a school bus is loading or unloading.

Alamo Rent-a-Car is one of the most popular car hire firms in Florida, but other companies such as Avis, Budget, Hertz, Dollar and Thrifty also have a major presence. Each offers its own packages and discounts, but in any case car hire is cheaper in this state than in any other. It should be noted that car rental companies will *not* accept cash – you will need one of the major credit cards. Some operators feature fly/drive programmes here, often including use of a car for a specific period. However, do ensure that the size of vehicle being offered is suitable for you – a family of four will not be comfortable on a long trip in a 'compact'; it might be better to pay extra for a larger model. Collision Damage Waiver (CDW) insurance, is usually an 'extra', though it is strongly recommended; otherwise in the event of an accident you will be liable for the cost of repairs up to the full value of the car.

Beware, Florida possesses inaptly named 'lovebugs' – extremely sticky and acidic insects that swarm during daylight hours in spring and autumn, clogging radiators and windscreens. During these times restrict driving to early morning or late afternoon and drive at lower speeds.

Bus Greyhound Lines operates an inter-city service between many Florida cities. Anyone considering using this mode of transport a great deal should think about purchasing an Ameripass (only available outside the US, for details in the UK, tel: 01342 317317). Passes are for 7 days, 15 days or 30 days – unlimited daily extensions are available at the time of purchase of the Ameripass. Passes enable visitors to travel anywhere over Greyhound's entire route system.

Local communities, including the major cities of Miami, Orlando and Tampa are served by local buses. Miami, in addition, is served by an elevated metrorail service into the downtown area connecting to an automated People Mover rail line. Tampa too has a People Mover rail line connecting the business district with Harbour Island.

Taxis These are plentiful, and except for airport zone trips, operate on a metered basis. If vacant (with the light on), they may be hailed on the street, or phoned for, or found in ranks in city centres and outside major hotels. Taxis charge a fixed flat rate, plus an additional fee based on distance. In Miami they can be expensive.

Rail Inter-city rail service, with Miami station its southernmost point, is provided by America's National Railroad Corporation, Amtrak. A special Florida 15- or 30-day Rail Pass is available for purchase prior to departure outside the US (for details in the UK, tel: (0171) 978 5212). A valid passport is required at the time of purchase. These passes may also be bought in Florida.

Electricity

The standard electricity supply in the US is 110 volts (60 cycles). You may have to bring an adaptor to convert. The sockets fit plugs with two flat pins. Appliances without dual voltage capability will also need a transformer. Your hotel will be able to give information if necessary.

Emergency Telephone Number

Phone 911 (the call is free), then ask for the service you require.

Health

It cannot be emphasised enough that arranging medical insurance before travelling is essential. Medical facilities are generally of an extremely high standard but costs in the US are exorbitant so it is imperative that you take out insurance cover beforehand. An insurance cover for an unlimited amount of medical costs is recommended. Treatment (unless an emergency) will be refused without evidence of insurance, or a deposit. If you need a doctor during your stay, ask at your hotel or look in the Yellow Pages under 'Physician'. (See also **Pharmacist**, below).

No inoculations are required for a visit to Florida, but it is a rabies risk area. Tap water is generally considered safe to drink.

Holidays – Public

New Year's Day (1 January)
Martin Luther King Day (15 January)
Washington's Birthday (third Monday in February)
Good Friday

Memorial Day (last Monday in May)
Independence Day (4 July)
Labor Day (first Monday in September)
Columbus Day (second Monday in October)
Veterans' Day (11 November)
Thanksgiving Day (fourth Thursday in November)
Christmas Day.

International Motoring Benefits

The American Automobile Association (AAA) is a member of the worldwide association of motoring organisations – the International Touring Alliance (AIT) – and as such makes certain services available to visitors of member organisations. The level of service differs between member organisations, so check eligibility with your own club. The AAA *cannot* deal directly with your enquiries before you leave; your own club should help with travel information and routes. Once you have arrived in the US, however, there are AAA offices in most large towns, ports and airports offering travel related assistance. You must produce a valid AIT-affiliated certificate to ensure free service.

Emergency Road Service

The AAA operates a nationwide emergency road service number to assist you in case of difficulties with your car. If you require assistance while travelling in the US, call 1-800-222-7764 and you will be given information for obtaining emergency assistance. If you are involved in a traffic accident it must be reported to the local police station, County

Sheriff's Office, or Florida Highway Patrol at once.

Money Matters

As a general rule, banks are open from 09.00 to 15.00 hrs Monday to Friday, and are closed on weekends and public holidays, although in some major towns and tourist areas hours may be longer. Currency may be changed at airports and hotels, but it is best to take US dollar travellers' cheques (travellers' *checks*, in the US). The advantage of this is that US dollar travellers' cheques can be used very much like cash. Hotels, restaurants, petrol stations and shops in Florida will accept them as cash and give change where necessary. It is a useful way of topping up your cash supply without going to the bank (in any case, many banks do not have the facility to encash travellers' cheques, and those that do are likely to charge a high commission). For this reason it is advisable to take out travellers' cheques in denominations of $10 or $20. The American monetary unit is of course the dollar, which is divided into 100 cents. The usual coins are the one cent (or penny), the five cent (nickel), the 10 cent (dime) and the 25 cent (quarter). There are also half-dollar and one-dollar coins. Try and keep some small change ready at all times as some public transport and telephones may require exact amounts. Notes (bills) are issued in denominations of 1, 2, 5, 10, 20, 50 and 100 dollars. Be warned, though: all notes, whatever their value, are *exactly the same colour and size*. The easiest bills to work with are the $10 and $20, with a few singles for tipping. Remember that each American state levies a tax on goods (except 'necessary' food purchased in grocery stores), so the price tag you see may not be the price you pay. In Florida's case, the sales tax is currently 6 per cent. An additional Resort Tax applies to hotels and restaurants, and sometimes a convention tax is levied on hotels. Rates vary between municipalities, but the final bill could have up to 11 per cent added in tax.

You can use credit cards almost anywhere. All the major cards are accepted throughout Florida.

If you run out of money, consult the Yellow Pages for foreign exchange brokers or head for American Express. There are no currency limitations (see **Customs Regulations**).

Pharmacist

Proprietary medicines are readily available at any pharmacy (drug store). Drug stores also sell a wide range of other goods including magazines, stationery etc.

Places of Worship

Churches of all denominations will be found in the major cities. Check times of services and locations in local newspapers or with hotels.

Post Office

Post office hours are generally Monday to Friday 09.00–17.00hrs and Saturday 9.00hrs–noon, but these do vary both in central city branches and in small towns, so it is best to check locally. Stamps, however, may be purchased in hotels, motels, drug stores and transport terminals, usually by inserting correct change into a machine, though these charge 25 per cent more.

Publications

There are countless free 'What's On'-type magazines and newssheets for holiday-makers, stuffed full of advertisements and money-off coupons. Look out for the Friday edition of the local paper, particularly in Orlando and Miami, for a more objective review of events and attractions over the weekend and forthcoming week.

Senior Citizens

Florida probably attracts more elderly people than any other state, and although senior citizen discounts are common throughout the state, they are not clearly displayed. Your best bet is simply to ask whether there is a senior citizen discount available on any purchase, meal, or hotel/motel stay.

Sport and Recreation

Florida is a very sporty state, for both participants and spectators and pastimes are diverse enough to suit any taste. Among the most popular spectator sports are the motor races in Daytona Beach, horse racing at Hialeah (Miami), jai-alai in

Miami, and American football. The rodeos at Kissimmee, Homestead and Arcadia are state events. There are plenty of dog racing tracks throughout the state. For participatory sports, Florida specialises in the water variety. With miles of inland and coastal waterways and innumerable marinas, boating of all kinds is a way of life, from canoeing to cruising. The Florida Canoe Trail System encompasses 35 rivers and waterways.

There are unlimited possibilities for fishing and underwater exploration. Many resort properties offer a full range of watersports and equipment rental, which often includes instruction, as well as facilities for other sports, such as horse back riding, tennis and golf. Hiking is also a very popular pastime, with ample opportunities for people of all ages and experience in Florida's many state parks.

Student and Youth Travel
Some operators specialise in travel for young people and/or exchange programmes. Florida has youth hostels in Clearwater Beach, Daytona Beach, Fort Lauderdale, Miami Beach, St Augustine and

Sea and sunshine make Florida the ideal state for water sports

St Petersburg. Book ahead if travelling in high season. Some attractions offer a special admission price for students and there are student concessions for some regular rail fares.

Telephones

Exact change in 5c, 10c and 25c pieces is needed except in an emergency, when you should dial the operator (just dial '0'). Alternatively, you could apply for a BT charge card, which is atutomatically billed to your account. Florida has a direct-dial system divided into four telephone regions, with the area codes of 305, 831, 407 and 904. To make a 'zone call' (*ie* call long distance within the same area code), dial 1 plus telephone number. To call outside the area code, dial 1, plus area code, plus telephone number. For direct dialling international calls dial 011, plus country code, plus city code (omit the initial 0 or 9; 15 or 16 for France), plus telephone number. If you use your hotel room phone, expect to pay a premium. For calls placed between 17.00 and 23.00 hrs there is a cheaper rate, and calls are cheaper still between 23.00 and 08.00 hrs and at weekends.

Time

Most of Florida is on Eastern Standard Time for much of the year – 5 hours behind Britain, 6 hours behind the rest of Western Europe and 15 hours behind Australia (Sydney).

Part of the northwest, including Pensacola and Fort Walton Beach is on Central Time, an hour behind the rest of Florida.

Tipping

Tipping is common practice in the US. The majority of hotels in Florida do not include a service charge in their bills (different from tax, see **Money Matters**). As a general rule visitors should tip porters 50 cents–$1 per bag; taxi drivers, 15 per cent of fare; hotel chambermaids, 50–70c per night; and in restaurants or hairdressers, 15 per cent of the bill.

Toilets

Public toilets, usually only found within airports, bus and train stations, are almost always of a high standard. They are known as 'Rest Rooms', and are usually free. Colloquially a toilet is called a 'john' in America.

Tourist Offices

The Florida Division of Tourism has a London office (tel: (0171) 727 8854). In Florida contact: Office of Visitor Inquiry, Florida Division of Tourism, Collins Building,126 West Gaines Street, Tallahassee, FL 32399-2000 (tel: (904) 488 7598). The Florida Division of Tourism operates visitor centres in major towns and resorts and at several roadside locations. For more specific information, ask for the local tourist office in the area you wish to visit.

INDEX

accommodation 24–5, 35, 42, 54, 64–5, 72, 114
air travel 11, 119
Alligatorland Safari Zoo 44
Amelia Earhart Park 13
Amelia Island 73
Apalachicola 73–4
Apopka 44
Arabian Nights 44
Arch Creek Park 13
Art Deco District 12, 13–15, 24–5

banks 123
Bass Museum 15
Bayfront Park 11, 15
bed and breakfast 35, 114
Big Pine Key 32
Black Island 37
Boca Raton 74, 76
Bonita Beach 37–8
Busch Gardens 69–71
buses 121–2

Cabbage Island 38
Caladesi Island 56
Calle Ocho 15, 111, 113
camping 35, 119
Cape Canaveral National Seashore 76
Cape Coral 38
Captiva Island 38–9
car hire 118, 121
Cauley Square 15
Cayo Costa 39
Central Florida Railroad Museum 44
Central Florida Zoo 44
children's activities 25, 35–6, 42, 49–53, 65, 72, 115–6
Clearwater 56–7
Clermont 45
climate 115
clothing 115
Cocoa Beach 76–7
Coconut Grove 16
Coral Castle 17
Coral Gables 17

countryside and wildlife 101–9
customs regulations 120
Cypress Gardens 45–6

Dade City 77
Dania Beach 77
Daytona Beach 77
Deerfield Beach 77–8
De Land 78
Delray Beach 78
discounts and budget tips 118, 124, 125–6
Disney-MGM Studios 51–2
Disney World see Walt Disney World
driving 121, 123
Dunedin 57–8

electricity voltage 122
emergency telephone numbers 122, 123
EPCOT 50–1
Estero Island 39
Everglades 78–80, 102–5, 106–7

Fairchild Tropical Gardens 18
festivals and events 13, 15, 16, 32–3, 58, 69, 78, 116–17
Flamingo Park 18
food and drink 110-11
forests 106-7, 108
Fort Lauderdale 81–3
Fort Myers 39–40
Fort Pierce 83
Fort Walton Beach 83
Freedom Tower 18
Fruit and Spice Park 18

Gainesville 83
Gasparilla Island 41
Gatorland Zoo 46, 51
Gold Coast Railroad & Museum 18

Harry P Leu Gardens 46
Haulover Park 19
Health Matters 122, 124
Hialeah Park 20

history of region 7–8, 9–11, 29, 68
Holiday Isles 58–9
Hollywood 83–4
Homosassa Springs 84–5
Honeymoon Island 59
hotels see accommodation

insurance, medical 122
Islamorada 31–2

Jacksonville 85
Jupiter 86–7

Kennedy Park 20
Kennedy Space Center/Spaceport USA 86–7
Key Biscayne 20
Key Largo 30–1
Key West 32–5
The Keys 29–36, 107, 111
Kissimmee 46

Lake Wales 46
Largo 59
Lee Island Coast 37–42
Lower Keys 32–5
Lowry Park Zoo 71
Lummus Park 20

Madeira Beach 59–60
Metro-Dade Cultural Center 21
Metrozoo 21–2
Miami 8, 9–28
Miami Museum of Science and Space Transit Planetarium 22
Miami Seaquarium 22
Miami Youth Museum 22
Miccosukee Indian Village 22
Middle Keys 32
money 123–4
Monkey Jungle 22–3
Monticello 87–8

nightlife 114

INDEX

Ocala National forest 88
Original Orchid Jungle 23
Orlando (city) 46–8
Orlando and vicinity 43–54
Osceola National Forest 88

Palm Beach 8, 88–90
Panama City 90
Parrot Jungle and Gardens 23
passports/visas 119
Pensacola 90–2
Pine Island 41
The Pinellas 55–65
Pompano Beach 92–3
ponds and lakes 105–6
public holidays 122–3

rail travel 122
restaurants 26, 36, 42, 54, 65, 72

Safety Harbor 60
St Augustine 93–6, 111
St Pete Beach 60
St Petersburg 60–3
Sanibel Island 41–2
Sarasota 96–8
Sea World 48
self-catering 114
shells 38, 40, 41–2, 108–9
shopping 26–8, 36, 42, 54, 65, 72, 112–14
Silver Springs 49
Singer Island 96
South Pointe Park 23
Spanish Monastery 23
Splendid China 49
sport and recreation 124–5
swamps 108

Tallahassee 98–100
Tampa 8, 55, 66–72
Tarpon Springs 63–4, 111, 114

taxis 122
telephones 126
time, local 126
tipping 126
toilets 126
tourist offices 126
Treasure Island 64

Universal Studios 49
Upper Keys 31–2
Useppa Island 42

Vizcaya 23

Walt Disney World 5–6, 47, 49–53
Water Mania 53
Weeki Wachee Spring 100
Weeks Air Museum 23
Wet'n'Wild 53–4
wildlife 78–80, 101–9

Ybor City 72, 111, 113

The Automobile Association would like to thank the following photographers and libraries for their assistance in the compilation of this book.

AA PHOTO LIBRARY 45 Cypress Gardens, 47 Magic Kingdom Walt Disney World, 51 Splash Mountain Walt Disney World & 52 Disney -MGM Studios (A Souter), 48 Sea World (P Bennett)

J ALLAN CASH PHOTOLIBRARY 14 Art Deco, Miami, 16 Vizcaya Mansion, 21 Key Biscayne, 22 Seaquarium, 30/1 Key Largo, 39 Edison Museum, 41 Sanibel Island, 59 Madeira Beach, 62/3 Sponges at Tarpon Springs, 72 Kapok Tree Restaurant, 76 Canaveral wildlife reserve, 84 Remains of sugar cane mill, 86/7 Jupiter Island, 89 Flagler Museum, 89 Door ornament, 92/3 St Augustine, 95 St Augustine Church, 112 HMS Bounty.

INTERNATIONAL PHOTOBANK 4 Disney World, 9 Miami Beach, 18 Bird of Paradise Flower, 35 Key West Church, 55 St Pete Beach, 56/7 Clearwater Beach, 61 St Petersburg, 64 Hotel Don Cesar, 69 Busch Gardens, The Python, 80 Anhinga Trail, 101 Fairchild Tropical Gardens, 116 Macaw.

NATURE PHOTOGRAPHERS LTD 104 Heron, 107 Great white heron, 109 Barred owl, Screw Pines (Paul Sterry).

SPECTRUM COLOUR LIBRARY 6 EPCOT Center, 7 Indian statue, 25 Parrot Jungle, 33 Hemingway House, 36 Fishing, 53 Wet 'n' Wild, 70/1 Busch Gardens, 79 Snake-bird, 82 Yachts, 94 Castillo de San Marcos, 100 Kennedy Space Center, 102/3 Alligator, 110 Oranges, 120 Rent a Car, 125 Windsurfing, Florida Keys.

ZEFA PICTURE LIBRARY UK LTD Cover Miami, Art Deco, 12 Miami, 27 Bayside Market, 29 Florida Keys, 81 Fort Lauderdale, 96/7 Sarasota, 98/9 Tallahassee.

Contributors

For this revision

Copy editors: Claire Watkins & Colin Follett   Researcher/verfier: Paul Murphy